To Father Ray
with The love of
Jesus,

maria.

Augustinian Inst. Villanova,
1984

Faith Is Friendship

Acknowledgments

All photographs by Joseph DeCaro
except page XVII - Kanisius Verlag
pp. XI, 51, 67, 99 - Jeffrey Mickler, SSP

Photo Editors: Jeffrey Mickler, SSP
                  Frank Sadowski, SSP

Faith Is Friendship

Josef Heinzmann

Translated by David Heinzmann

ALBA · HOUSE · NEW · YORK

SOCIETY OF ST. PAUL, 2187 VICTORY BLVD., STATEN ISLAND, NEW YORK 10314

Library of Congress Cataloging in Publication Data

Heinzmann, Josef.
  Faith is friendship.

  Translation of: Glauben ist Freundschaft.
  1. Faith—Meditations. 2. Meditations. I. Title.
BV4637.H4413   1983   234'.2   83-15376
ISBN 0-8189-0451-8

Nihil Obstat:
Michael J. Wrenn, M.A., M.S.
Censor Librorum

Imprimatur:
† Joseph T. O'Keefe, D.D.
Vicar General, Archdiocese of New York
September 8, 1983

Designed, printed and bound in the United States of
America by the Fathers and Brothers of the
Society of St. Paul, 2187 Victory Boulevard,
Staten Island, New York 10314, as part of their
communications apostolate.

---

1 2 3 4 5 6 7 8 9 (Current Printing: first digit)

Table of Contents

FOREWORD IX

INTRODUCTION XIII
0. Man, Seeker After God XIII
   0.1 Man, who are you? XIII
   0.2 Man: where from, where to, and why? XVIII
   0.3 On the trail of the infinite XXIII

PART ONE:
CHRISTIAN FAITH IS FAITH IN A PERSON 3
1. Knowing God: In And With The Heart (Familiarity With God) 3
   1.1 Credo: I give my heart 3
   1.2 Believing in a thing 4
   1.3 Faith in a Person 5
   1.4 Faith as invitation and encounter 7
   1.5 Faith as gift and promise 8
   1.6 Faith as "acquaintance" with God 11

2. Knowing God: Knowing Who He Is (Image Of God) 11
   2.1 Divine revelation 11
   2.2 The experience of God 12
   2.3 The image of God 15
   2.4 Talking about God 17
   2.5 The personal God 18
   2.6 The living God 18
   2.7 The loving God 20
   2.8 God, coming and already nigh 23

3. Knowing God: Knowing What He Does
   (The Mighty Deeds Of God) 25
   3.1 The wonderful works of God 25
   3.2 Creation 25
   3.3 The Incarnation 32
   3.4 Jesus Christ the Redeemer 34
   3.5 Death and Resurrection 37

4. Knowing God: Knowing What He Says (God's Word) 42
    4.1 Word as encounter 42
    4.2 The Word of God 42
    4.3 The Incarnate Word of God 43
    4.4 God's Word in writing 43
    4.5 "Words taught by the Spirit" 45
    4.6 God's Word in human words 46

5. Recognizing God (Encounter With God) 49
    5.1 "Know the Lord" 49
    5.2 Sacraments: signs of faith 54
    5.3 Baptism: children of God 59
    5.4 Eucharist: meeting the Lord 59
    5.5 Penance: friendship lives on forgiveness 61
    5.6 Prayer: lived friendship 62

6. Knowing And Recognizing God (Gratitude And Witness) 66
    6.1 Everything is Faith 67
    6.2 Do not be afraid 70
    6.3 Wonder 74
    6.4 Joy 76
    6.5 The revolutionary Sermon on the Mount 79
    6.6 Gratitude 81
    6.7 Festivity 81
    6.8 Testimony 82
    6.9 The missionary call 85

PART TWO:
CHRISTIAN FAITH IS ORIENTED TOWARDS COMMUNITY 89
7. Fraternal Faith 89
    7.1 We believe 90
    7.2 Credo as symbol 90
    7.3 Christ our brother 91
    7.4 A people of believers 91
    7.5 Faith: conceived in community 92
    7.6 Faith: nourished in the community 93
    7.7 Faith: community oriented 96
    7.8 "Serve one another in love" 100

PART THREE:
CHRISTIAN FAITH IS WORLD-ORIENTED 105
8. Faith Open To The World 105

8.1 The world: temptation or way to God? 105
8.2 Infatuated with the world 106
8.3 God's gift to the world 106
8.4 Church for the world 107
8.5 Steward and shaper of creation 108
8.6 The purpose of work 109
8.7 Progress and technology 111
8.8 Christian responsibility for the world 112
8.9 "Justice and peace shall kiss" 114

PART FOUR:
CHRISTIAN FAITH IS HISTORY-ORIENTED 117
9. Historical faith 117
9.0 The mystery of time 117
9.1 History: sister of time 119
9.2 God's history with man 119
9.3 Underway in faith 123
9.4 Final destination: death? 126
9.5 The future has already begun 131
9.6 "Eternally with the Lord" 134
9.7 The "new earth" 139
9.8 Faith in today 141

CONCLUSION:
ARRIVING AT THE GOAL 145
9.9 Mary: A model of faith 145

FOREWORD

0.0.1 Friendship. This bold and tender picture shows St. John's love for Jesus. John is resting his head upon Jesus' heart. The Beloved Disciple's eyes are closed. "I sleep, but my heart is awake" (Sg 5:2). Oblivious of everything about him, he can listen with ever greater intensity. "Faith comes from hearing" (Rm 10:17). Totally immersed in the other. Self-surrender. Words are superfluous. The only speech that passes his lips is a restrained smile. Christ allows St. John to do as he pleases. In fact, he even rests his arm on his friend's shoulder. The Redeemer's eyes are looking into the distance—at once an invitation and a question: "Are we really friends?"

0.0.2 Faith is Friendship! The title of this book might seem unusual and something of a surprise. It is just as surprising as our Lord's avowal: "I call you friends" (Jn 15:15). In the many centuries since Christ's birth, countless people have been fascinated by this friendship with Christ. St. Paul considers everything as rubbish in comparison to it (Ph 3:8). "I know in whom I have placed my trust" (2 Tm 1:12). On the basis of his own personal experience the Apostle dares to offer this reckless challenge: "Accept the friendship that God is offering to you" (2 Cor 5:20).

0.0.3 Faith is Friendship! This was the mystery of the saints, the mystery on which they lived. For them Christ was not a "problem," but Lord and Friend. To be sure, faith in Christ has never been easy. Following the Crucified Lord always calls for sacrifice and for shedding blood. And yet this friendship with the Risen Savior has, for many people, transformed sadness into joy, and meaninglessness into inspired enthusiasm.

0.0.4 Faith is Friendship! But why, today, have so many Christians lost this joy in their faith, this joy which comes from faith? There are many reasons. The insipid character of contemporary life and a world out of joint do not make faith a simple undertaking. There are many things today which make faith hard to find: the general preoccupation with performance, so-called secularization, the widespread intellectual crisis. The roots of this evil, however, lie much deeper. It is not that Christ and his Gospel have become something empty and worn out. No, it is rather our faith that seems to be sick. Are we not threatened by the danger of camouflaging and thus betraying the "Gospel core," to such a degree that we see Christianity as only a handy catalogue of obligations and commandments and truths? Of pushing Christ back and forth in our heads for so long, that he has become a mere object of speculation? Of rethinking his good news into such a disfigured travesty that it turns into an inexhaustible mine of "problems"?

In a word, haven't we made Christianity too much an affair of duty and mind? Conceived in this light, Christian faith turns into a grotesque caricature. Such a degenerate form of Gospel cannot possibly offer any inspiration to people today—especially young people. There can be no incentive to dedicate one's life for an ideal like this, to live and die for it. A faith like that would be considerably out of harmony with our human experience.

0.0.5 Faith is Friendship! This is not a question of pursuing the conflict between understanding and feeling. What I mean is this: faith is not primarily a matter of the head or the understanding, but of the heart and the whole man. Heart, in the Biblical sense of the word, signifies the most profound and noble element in the human person, his innermost mystery, the place where a human being is really and truly a human being. "Man looks upon the face, but the Lord looks into the heart" (1 S 16:7). The decisive element is "what comes out of the heart" (Lk 6:45). The New Testament speaks of "the Holy Spirit who is poured out into our heart" (Rm 5:5), of the "eyes of the heart" (Ep 1:18) with which we can grasp "the good news of God which is in our heart" (Rm 10:8). Antoine de Saint-Exupéry puts it best in his well-known statement that man can see well only with his heart. St. Paul sums it up boldly and precisely: "Man believes with his heart" (cf. Rm 10:10). *Credo,* the Latin word for *believe,* is equivalent to "I surrender my heart" (*credere = cor dare =* to give one's heart).

0.0.6 Faith is Friendship! An essential and fundamental ingredient of Christian faith is the personal experience that takes place in the innermost core of the human soul: the loving self-surrender and bond with Another. Faith is thus primarily an "affair of the heart." "If you seek me with your whole heart, I will let you find me" (Jr 29:13-14). The reverse is also true: "He who does not love, does not know God" (1 Jn 4:8). To live on terms of intimate love with God, to entrust ourselves in faith and confidence to the whole story of God with man, to commit ourselves wholly to Christ—this is the basic core of Christian faith.

0.0.7 Faith is Friendship! Faith is not complicated. It is just as simple as loving each other is for two people in love. It is only when we improperly analyze the basic experience of faith, when we start to dissect it into tiny pieces and put words to everything, that it becomes hopelessly complicated and lifeless. If you take a living body and cut it into pieces, the body dies. This is true even if you did so only in an effort to know and understand it better. Living and loving and believing are all things that operate as a unity, a totality. They are immeasurably more than even the most comprehensive understanding and knowledge about life and love and faith.

0.0.8 Faith is Friendship! And thus we have already stated the fundamental thesis of this book, seen in its most essential outlines. It is not my purpose here to write a learned and theoretical treatise on the subject of faith. In fact, it is precisely this problematical approach to the subject, so characteristic of our modern outlook, that I have deliberately tried to avoid. Questioning and analyzing and complaining and accusing—there is more than enough of that today. And from that point of view this little book is incomplete and one-sided.

On the other hand, it is certainly not my intention to foster the development of religious fanaticism, or to overplay the actual difficulties inherent in believing. All I want to do is to accentuate the element of giving and the element of happiness about our faith. Can this succeed? All our talk about God and his history with men is and remains a helpless stammering. What we mean is always infinitely more exalted than what we can say.

But despite all this, I hope that I shall be able to offer some modest help to a few people who have either not yet discovered Christianity or who have been disillusioned by it, to make it easier for them to experience the joy that comes from believing. It is thus a sort of pastoral book, a book of faith; but at the same time it is a book of confession and contemplation. For every time we talk about God, there must be a confession, an overwhelming experience of conviction.

0.0.9 It was in Latin America that I made the decision to write this book. There I met so many poor campesinos, plain working men, simple Indians. Many of them had never seen the inside of a school and could neither read nor write. But they had managed to develop the talents of their heart to an enviable degree. I was often forced to marvel at the simplicity and directness of their faith in their Redeemer Christ. How often was I ashamed to witness the wisdom of their hearts, their way of "knowing about Christ." Often I have had to ask myself who could have been their teacher in faith. Involuntarily the words of Jesus would come to mind: "Father, I thank you that you have revealed these things to the little ones" (Mt 11:25).

Faith is Friendship
Prof. Josef Heinzmann, Redemptorist
Klemensheim 3953 Leuk-Stadt

INTRODUCTION

0. MAN, SEEKER AFTER GOD

0.1 Man, who are you?

0.1.0 Man, who or what are you? Ever since you have lived on earth, ever since you have been able to think and to investigate, you have been occupied with this question: who or what am I, really? A riddle? A mystery? A miracle? The result of chance? A missing link? Or simply a fascinating question to which there is no real answer?

You know a great deal about yourself, and you are always learning more. You have deciphered the riddle of your body, piece by piece. You know how it originates and grows, and how its organs function. You know the chemical formulas for flesh and bone. But has all this really brought you to grips with the ultimate mystery?

0.1.1 Man: a frightening marvel. You are curious about yourself. In the quiet hours you seek after yourself, listen to your hidden depths, reflect about your innermost being. It is then that you are gripped by a sudden wonder at your own ultimate mystery. And it frightens you. You are capable of joy and faithfulness, forgiveness and hope. You can think and plan and speak. You have succeeded in translating your enthusiasm and your inspiration, your suffering and your sorrows, into magnificent works of art. You can build domes and invent computers.

In your innermost soul, question after question arises. They are a stimulus for your activity, but you can never answer all of them. You delve into questions of where you come from and where you are going, but your journeys into the past and into the future never reach their goal.

Your heart is crying out for happiness, but you are insatiable in your longing. A whole lifetime is not enough to quiet the unbounded desires of your heart.

But what shall we say about your most precious talent, your ability to love? In a thousand ways you have celebrated the wonder of love in song and poetry, and still you have never even glimpsed what love really is. In a million ways you have known love, and yet every new love is something so precious and tender and fresh and young, that it seems you have discovered love for the very first time. It is something never used up or worn out. Your heart always wants the same thing: a sense of self-giving, being understood, being accepted. In a word, love.

You have been created for friendship. But friendship is always and essentially a free offer and invitation, never pressure and compulsion. An essential element of friendship is always the risk involved in freedom.

Man, you are a frightening marvel! So unique, so irreplaceable, so inexhaustible, so simply wonderful. We can pronounce your name only with the greatest reverence, even though it is a name that has been horribly defiled.

0.1.2 Man, a tattered bit of unhappiness? You have been cast into existence. You were never able to make a decision for or against life. No one ever even asked you. And still you are plagued all your life by the question of why you were ever born.

All during your life you are exposed, threatened and in jeopardy. In the jungle of your heart there are always so many cares and concerns: anxiety about life and death, anxiety about the past and the future. Doubt and failure are often your guests, and you live in a state of war with yourself. Mistrust of your own self can cripple you, torture your soul, even destroy you completely.

With every fiber of your being you cry out for community and communication. You are packed together with masses of people: in the sports stadium, at the beach, in traffic jams and tenement houses. And still you are so often lonesome and alone, sometimes to the point of despair and even suicide.

Whoever gave you the gift of freedom entered into an unbelievable risk together with you, by the very fact of that gift. You can misuse the gift and injure other people. You are capable of spite and malice and the most despicable offenses. Poverty, hate and enmity, worldwide hunger, pillage, war, violence and rape, terror and criminal behavior, deportation, concentration camps, torture, murder and mass murder—these words set in motion an endless horror film before our minds.

Disease can also shatter human happiness in so many ways. Every hospital is the symbol of this fact. The sanitarium is an accumulation of suffering and misery, not only for the sick themselves, but also for their families, their friends and acquaintances. When the sick gnash their teeth for pain or crouch like worms; when they are lying there exhausted by lack of blood or shaking with fever; when they are gasping and fighting for air or the rattle of death is in their throats; when we witness the last convulsions of a man who has been consumed by fire or mangled in some grisly accident—then we might well be inclined to ask ourselves if man is really anything more than a tattered bit of misery.

0.1.3 Man, your life is ticking away. The world is full of clocks. You can hardly imagine modern living without these measurements of time. Seconds pass into minutes, minutes into hours, hours into days, days into weeks, months, years, decades, centuries, millennia. Past, present and future all flow imperceptibly together. Mystery of time and history!

You alone, man, of all creatures, know about past and future. Like a miniature building block you are born into a specific day in a specific year, and thus into one specific point in the whole history of the world and humankind.

By this very fact, you have been firmly rooted into past generations. Your ancestors and parents passed on their heritage from one generation to another, all the way down to you. From the very first moment of your life, you have been inextricably woven into the warp and woof of the millions of people of yesteryear and today. You are still just an innocent child in the uncomplicated world of childhood (which is also a visible sign of the fact that God has not yet lost his enjoyment of humankind), and already you are bound up with fate, both with the greatest plans of mankind and also with its most killing miseries.

You are on your way in the company of many others. Most of them are not related to you, and still they are all of the same human blood. You are unique, and yet your history is rooted firmly in a countless array of human destinies.

Indeed, your life is ticking away. Your time is passing. But all your experiences and discoveries, all your insights and accomplishments, are not simply once and for all past and forgotten. In a mysterious manner they are all alive, and their effects continue in the depths of your psyche. Nobody can find his way in the confusing network of the human soul, in the ins and outs of the deepest core of the human self. Every moment of your life is carried along and somehow co-determined by your own past. All this you are carrying along with you into the future.

You are in love, infatuated with your own life's history. Somehow you bear within yourself the desire to endow it with substance and duration, in your children, in your work and in your monuments. Perhaps you are right. But is it worth the effort? Your life is ticking away, and even from your birth you are walking towards your death. A modern poet has expressed this experience in brutally graphic words:

> It takes nine months to create a human being, but a single day is enough to kill him. Both of us have experienced this often enough. But just listen now. It takes not nine months, but fifty years, to make a human being. Fifty years of sacrifices and so many other things. And when this man has finally been created, when there is nothing of childhood left within him, when he is finally a complete human person, then all he is good for is to die (André Malraux).

0.1.4 Man, kiss the earth. These are the words that the Virgin Mary is supposed to have spoken to Bernadette at Lourdes: "Kiss the earth." You, man, not only have a body; you are a body. It is precisely through this body that you are related to earth. The Bible pairs the name of the first human being (*adam* = man) with the word *adamah*, which means farmland. Since the Creator fashioned you from the material of the earth, you can no longer repudiate your earthly origins. Kiss the earth! In a symbolic gesture of love for the world. All things love each other; they form a solidarity among themselves and embrace each other. You too, man, must love them, and they love you. You are woven into the very fabric of the world. Their destiny is bound up with yours.

And you are the uncrowned king of all living creatures and all things. The Bible records that Adam gave a name to every creature. He was aware of his bond with them, and his dominion over them. You, man, can subject everything to yourself. Through your knowledge and technology you acquire more and more power over all visible creation. And still you cannot succeed in getting to the bottom. Every time you unravel one mystery, you are faced with ten other riddles.

The world is your home. You may be amazed at the fact that there is so much beauty in the world. It is wonderful to behold the colors of the flowers, the glory of the mountains. It is wonderful to smell and taste and feel. It is wonderful to touch the earth with your hands and to walk on it with your feet. Take care that the world of creation never loses its mystery for you.

You love this world—and perhaps this is precisely why a quiet sense of nostalgia sometimes steals into your heart. For you are a pilgrim here below and you have here "no lasting abode" (Heb 13:14). Together with you, all creation is groaning for the fullness of redemption (Rm 8:19-23).

0.1.5 Man, God is using your face. "What is man that you, O God, are mindful of him?" (Ps 8:5). You, man, are the glory of God. At the moment of creation, God has raised you totally into his own proximity. He created you in his own "image and likeness" (Gn 1:26-27). You are a relative of God. To you, his partner, he has entrusted the world, for you to administer it.

When, some two thousand years ago, the Word became Flesh (Jn 1:14), and became a child (Lk 2:7), God, in Christ, took on a human countenance. And thus, more fully than you could have ever anticipated, God has become your partner, your relative, your comrade and companion. God used your countenance.

In our world you see so many faces: a face in which anxiety lives, a face that is disfigured because it has been tortured, a face in which despair is the dominant force. Do you recognize Christ in this countenance? On the day of Judgment he will unmask himself, removing the veil from his face: "It was I" (Mt 25:40).

And here you touch upon your ultimate mystery, your supreme dignity: in Jesus Christ you are a child of God. Man, God is using your face—do not misuse it!

0.1.6 Meditation: Christ and Adam. Two figures side by side: Christ and Adam. Erect. Forward-looking. Christ's gaze embraces everything: mankind and history; good and evil; past and present and future. "He is the image of the invisible God, the First-born before all creation. . . . All things have been created through him and for him" (Col 1:15, 16b). His unspeaking lips reflect the words of God. A divine light is reflected from his noble forehead. His countenance radiates a divine clemency, friendship with every human person. A friendship that turns into an interior festival, in the sense that Roger Schutz describes it: "In order to live a festival, you need faces and expressions rather than words. The faces transmit friendship and friendship is the face of Christ. Nothing is more beautiful than a face which the battles of a lifetime have made translucent. There are only beautiful faces, whether they are sorrowful or radiant."

His face is friendship with every human person. His gaze is born in the heart to which his hand is pointing. In the love of his heart, this gaze embraces the future of man (on the left). The man, holding up his head, with his pointed chin and tightly pressed lips, walks purposefully along the path into the future. Christ accompanies him, recognized or unrecognized. He is offering his brother the gift of friendship, so that he will take on his features more and more, for "all things have been created unto him."

Will man, at the end of his sojourn on earth, be made into the same form as Christ? Will I be made into the same form as Christ? The answer remains open. All I can say is this: "I will praise the Lord with the face that he gave me." And I am responsible for my face! (Franz-Toni Schallberger).

> Man, you are a work of God. And so wait for the hand of your artist which makes everything at the right time, the right time for you who are being made. Bring a pliable and willing heart to meet with him, and preserve the form that the artist gave to you. Let yourself be formed, so that you do not harden and end up losing the trace of his fingers. If you preserve the imprint of his fingers in yourself, you will rise up to perfection. The art and skill of God have shaped the clay that you are. After he formed you out of the material of the earth, he will adorn you within and without with pure gold and silver. He will make you so beautiful that in the end he will long for you himself (Irenaeus of Lyons).

0.2 Man: where from, where to, and why?

0.2.0 "I come, I don't know where from. I am and don't know who. I live and don't know how long. I die and don't know when. I'm going and I don't know where. It's a wonder that I'm happy." This old folk saying has

managed to capture one of the oldest of human experiences, man's questions about origins and goals, about the basis and meaning of his life, in a simple and gripping formulation.

0.2.1 Selections from a diary: In a room in a skyscraper the police discovered the half-decomposed body of an elderly woman. On the table lay her diary. It was open to the last page. A trembling hand had entered these final words:

> Today I am very sad. I am alone. Like in a dead-end street, in which it is dark and from which there is no way out. When I die, nobody will miss me. I have no relatives left. Neither can I work any more. I am too tired and perhaps also too old. I let my life pass before my eyes. It looks like an incomprehensible film to me, without beginning and without end, like an unfinished book with several chapters. No one can understand what is written because the writing is illegible. Perhaps they never should have written the book.

The diary is fairly thick. On the first page apparently a child had written in an unformed hand: "My diary. I am going to write a diary. My girl friend is doing one too. 'Later on it will be interesting,' she said." This must have been many years ago. The pages are all yellowed and the letters have faded.

Let us page through this book of personal recollections:

Today I am ten years old. I got many presents. The prettiest one was a watch. That is dumb. My girl friend has a new coat. I'd like to have one just like it.

Astrid was crying today. She said that her parents didn't understand her any more. My parents are good to me. I am happy. But it's too bad that they don't let me go out very often at night. This afternoon we had our annual birthday get-together. We measured how big we were. That was fun. Sonja is an inch bigger. But of course she is also a little older than I am. I don't like to look at myself any more in the mirror. If only I were out of school already!

I feel really rotten. Today I leave boarding school. For ever. Now my life begins. My last essay was entitled "My Plans for the Future." The teacher was very satisfied; she gave me a good mark and smiled and said that I had great plans.

This is a day I will never forget. This is the first time I was with my boy friend. We love each other so much. He even gave me a record player. He's going to marry me and we're going to be happy. I would have liked it best if I could have been together with him for ever. But now I am all alone once more. The tears flow down my cheeks. But the memory is beautiful.

I've been married now for three years already! We are happy and we have a fine healthy child. Our house is small, of course, but we don't have to pay too much rent for it either. Naturally, it would be nicer if we had our own house.

Life is like a dream. My husband keeps getting one raise after another. He has really been successful. Now we have our own house. I got my driver's license, so I can go out with the car whenever I want to. We got the first TV in the neighborhood. The other women are jealous of me. But it is a shame that our only child died. Often I ask myself who we are really working for, after all. Often I am dissatisfied with my life. It all seems so empty and meaningless for me.

Today I am in despair. I really don't know why. There is plenty of money. I can do whatever I want for myself. I can go on vacations. But afterwards I am even lonelier. I am separated from my husband. The woman he had his affair with destroyed so much happiness. Now I am old and not so attractive. My health also leaves a lot to be desired. Sometimes I get the impression that I am groping about in a black and empty room. Is this life? How can I go on? I ask myself what I should have done differently. I have not done anything really evil. And still I often see myself as someone who has failed, almost like a big sinner who has done everything wrong. If only I were young again. How many things I would change! But now? I ask myself, do I still have the right to go on living. . . .

0.2.2 Our heart is restless. Man, how unlike a man you would be if you ceased from asking questions. Even as a child you confuse your parents with questions for which there is no answer. And when you lie, in your old age, upon your deathbed, these same questions are still wandering around unanswered in your restless heart. There are many concerns to keep you occupied day after day. One way or another, they all lead into the most vexing questions of your life: Why am I alive? Where do I come from? What does it all mean? These questions are not just dictated by a passing fancy. They are always there, above everything else. Your whole life long, you are like a child who keeps boring his parents with the same eternal questions: "And then? And then? And then???"

Your heart is full of desires. Without them you cannot live. You are never satisfied. As a child you long for toys, you dream of Christmas presents, look forward to the day when you will be grown up and can leave school. Later, too, you are always striving for something. Your thirst for happiness is never completely stilled. So long as you are still hungrily grasping for something, you have the feeling that it is worth it all to be alive. Even in sickness and poverty life seems to be worth living, so long as there is at least a crumb of hope for you to latch onto. Striving—achieving—new desires: life is an eternal sense of never being satisfied. And even eventually, one way or another, it all boils down to the ultimate question of what is the final meaning of my life?

A desire without fulfillment—is that your destiny? Or is all this simply a reminder of a lost Paradise? The poet sees your situation as that of a migratory bird who was born in a distant place. When the winter approaches, he feels a mysterious sense of restlessness; a call of a very special nature deep within his blood; a longing for the land of the springtime which he has never seen but towards which he nonetheless sets out.

0.2.3. The Meaning of Life. Your human life is beautiful. Who could deny it? When things are going well and you are fully occupied with your work, when you are living in peace and you are loved, then you are not inclined to ask many particular questions about the ultimate meaning of existence. You simply live your life.

But all this can suddenly change. Your attitude towards life is like a windmill. You get sick, or grow old; you experience some failure, or you are disillusioned in your love for some fellow human person. Then you carry great wounds deep within your heart. And suddenly you find yourself all alone, and there is no one to understand you. There is no good advice, and no solution to your problem. You are visited with anxiety and nausea and monotony and emptiness. You are prey to a sense of what a burden life has become, and how the bottom has suddenly been snatched away from things. You begin to feel like a bird that has fallen out of its nest, and is exposed without any protection to the harsh realities of the world. It is in situations like these, where you come face to face with your ultimate limitations, that you can easily break down. Or at least the experiences will leave a lasting scar upon your life.

Something similar can happen when you experience a feeling of the instability of human life. Death robs you of a dear companion. Standing at his or her coffin, you are suddenly seized by the question of origins and goals, of meaning and purpose in life. And this question, which attacks you so pitilessly, demands to be answered. For what good does it do to be on your way, if you do not know what is your goal? Surely the road is pointless if it does not reach its goal.

0.2.4 Crisis of soul: a sickness of our times? In answering these questions deep within the soul, people today are better prepared and at the same time more uncertain than those of earlier generations. It would seem that fewer and fewer people are coming to terms with their life. Their inner sense of emptiness is making them sick. But why precisely now?

In its advertising, the consumer world promises happiness and prosperity. Material goods continue to pile up. It would appear that our needs can be more easily satisfied and our wishes more quickly fulfilled. But why are you then caught up in such a crisis of the spirit? Are you perhaps oversatiated? Do you have to struggle too little in order to attain your goals? One thing is clear: an increase in consumer goods alone does not bring true happiness.

In contrast to the external situation, the inner values are represented as second-rank. And thus you run the risk of remaining on the surface of existence. Is it for lack of depth, or simply that you do not have the time for recollection and quiet?

A society oriented towards accomplishment forces you—at school, in sports, at your work—to do ever greater things. Does all this perhaps make your human existence more difficult? Perhaps Viktor Frankl hit the nail square on the head when he wrote:

> In contrast to the animal, there are no instincts that tell man what he has to do. And in contrast to the men of yesterday, there are no traditions to tell the man of today what he ought to do. Now, knowing neither what he must do or what he should do, he often seems to be basically unsure of what it is he wants to do. And thus he wants to do only what the others do: conformism. Or else he wants to do only what the others want to do, and want him to do: totalitarianism.

Perhaps the "emancipated" man of today has bound himself in his own chains?

One thing more. It is characteristic of our times to question everything, to pick it apart, to analyze. At the same time you have lost your sense for the greater continuity and context. And thus you must face this splintering of reality without comprehension, as if it were a pile of debris. You can no longer really succeed in glimpsing a sense of the whole, or in finding any enlightening answers to the questions of where we are from and where we are going and where is the meaning.

0.3 On the trail of the infinite

0.3.0 You make a bold claim upon life. You do not want to face the future blindly. Rather, you want to give your life some meaning.

0.3.1 Meaning is not self-evident. Have you not had the horrible experience of realizing that there is a great rift running across the world and across our human life? Millions are starving to death; innocent children are suffering and dying. Death shatters so much happiness and love. The "meaning" behind all this does not immediately strike the eyes. Eating, drinking, sleeping, working: this eternal monotony of life can often make you sick. On tiptoe creeps in the temptation to refuse to live a life whose meaning you no longer know. To ask whether life is not a journey upon which you should never have set out. Meaning is not self-evident.

And still you do encounter something meaningful. The world and the things in it are marvelously, wonderfully arranged: the construction of the atom, the orbits of the planets, the course of the seasons, the instincts of the animals. You alone, man, are the only one who can ask about meaning. If there were no meaning, then either you would have to be without this unquenchable longing for it—or else all your hoping and longing and wishing and life itself would be absurd.

0.3.2 Meaning is not acquired, but experienced. If you have money, today you can buy almost anything. But sense and meaning you cannot acquire for all the riches in the world. It cannot be made by any patent solution, nor can it be found anywhere ready-made or in any easy recipe. Meaning can only be experienced.

0.3.3 Meaning is not something once and for all. Few things in your human living are so threatened and so fragile as precisely this meaning. Accomplished goals and blows of fate, sickness and old age, and above all the encounter with death call this meaning into question. In the course of your life, it is not always the same thing that is meaningful and deserving of effort. You must always look for meaning all over again, feel and experience it. You can never, throughout your life, hold it in your grasp wholly and inalienably. You are always on the way towards meaning. The search for meaning is a lifelong task.

0.3.4 Meaning is to be found in the depths of our own heart. Meaning is like a sensitive child, shy and reserved. *(photo on right)* It neither behaves noisily nor bustles around on the surface. If you want to find it, you must descend deep into the innermost depths of your own heart. Meaning is not to be found in the perfect cuisine, nor in an insurance policy, nor in any external success. In the last analysis, you will find it only in the very middle of your own heart. Or, to put it in different words: your life has just as much meaning as you yourself give to it. Your life is meaningful when you live it in a meaningful way. That is why it is a highly personal mandate to give your life an overall sense and meaning. We are each of us the forger of our own happiness. And "man does not live by bread alone" (Mt 4:4).

0.3.5 Meaning means essentially friendship. "I am looking for friends." Meaning is something that you cannot generally give to yourself. You need someone else. It is in your relationship and encounter with him or her that you are most likely to find and nourish your own meaning. You

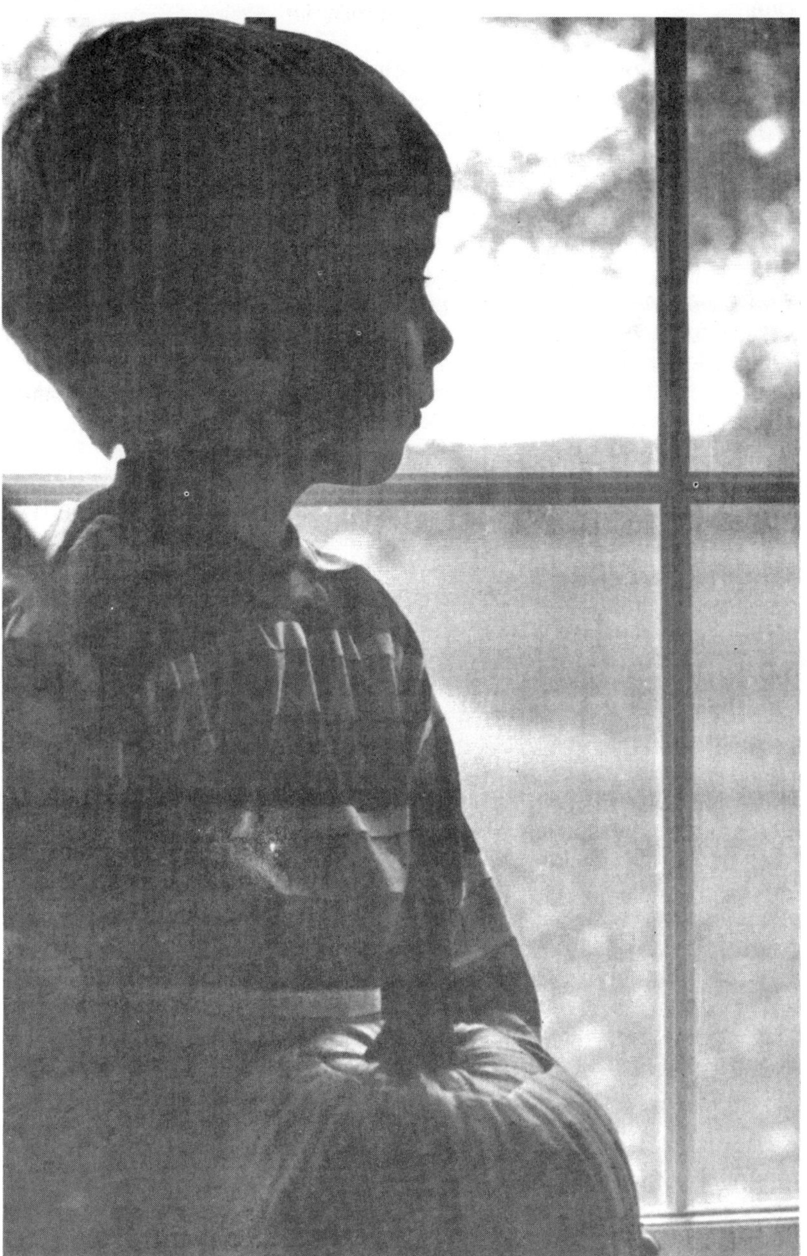

would like to be confirmed, endorsed and loved by someone else. In friendship, in married partnership and parenthood, you would like to experience being accepted by another. Love, security, recognition make your existence meaningful. Your home is not the place where you live, but the place where you are understood. "I am looking for friends." In these words Saint-Exupéry has captured the great longing of the human heart.

a. "It is not devotees I need, but friends." So many people are greedily chasing after honor and glory. They want to be admired and wondered at. The cult and uproar over beauty queens and movie stars is evidence enough. But how often these worshipped faces are dull and empty. They have lost their heart. In them the words of Kafka have been inscribed as upon a mask: "It is not devotees I want, but friends." Man is created for friendship like the bird for flying.

b. Friendship is love and trust. Friendship is something precious which can hardly be described. It is as mysterious as love and partnership could ever be. Friendship overcomes anxiety. You are not even afraid to lose yourself. You know that the other wants what is good for you. That he will neither use you nor abuse you. You can say everything to him and not be laughed at when you do. You can be the way you are and you will not be turned away. You can entrust yourself to your friend. Friendship is a splendid venture of love for a life full of trusting openness. It combines affection with respect and faithfulness.

c. Friendship is invitation and encounter. Love is not directed towards material things, but rather towards a living person. The mother cares for her child; the father works for his family; the nursing sister cherishes and cares for the dying patient; friends, man and woman, give each other little gifts as signs of tender affection. But friendship is never more than an invitation, a free offer. Force and pressure are quite alien to it. That is why you can dare to commit yourself so unreservedly to the other, to present him with the most precious element of your own person.

d. Friendship is gift and promise. True friendship does not know any boundary in time. It is meant to abide forever. Giving of self and allowing a gift to be made to self—this is an experience that longs to be repeated over and over again. Every surrender is more than a present that causes happiness. It is always a promise, too, which gives a further promise of new encounters. In this climate of security joy is born, and your true riches can develop and unfold. Hidden strengths that slumbered deep within you are awakened tenderly and almost without effort. Friendship makes you wealthy. It is a wonderland of surprises, an invitation to ever greater happiness; in a word, an unanticipated promise. That is why so many people see friendship as precisely the meaning of their lives. Meaning essentially involves friendship. "A true friend is a powerful protection; whoever finds him has great riches" (Si 6:14). 

0.3.6 Meaning reaches into the infinite. So many things can make you happy and give meaning to your life. You work and you get rich, and thereby you feel that you have established yourself. You start out on a beautiful journey or listen to some enchanting music, and these experiences cause you joy. As a young mother you embrace your child for the first time, or as a young lover you embrace your beloved: a transport of tremendous astonishment courses through your being. You are meeting with a person who loves you not for your beauty or your wealth, but simply because you are "you": this friendship transforms your life. You make the blessed discovery that "it is worthwhile to live; it is good that I am here. My life has meaning."

But can these magnificent experiences be the ultimate meaning of your life? Over everything lies the breath of the past. The music dies away. The most splendid trips and the most intoxicating embraces come to an end. Success and wealth are short-lived. Love, too, can suddenly die, when the beloved proves untrue or is torn from your side. And yet what you are looking for in friendship is something unqualified, something perfect. You wish that the happiness of love would never come to an end. And thus love leads to something over and above itself, the infinite.

You would like to live. To live forever. In your children, in your works, in your reputation you would like to preserve something of yourself over into eternity. And yet your life simply will not entirely succeed. It remains a fragment, just an artist's preliminary sketch. And then comes death. It comes to you. To everyone. And thus apparently everything that you have longed for and worked for is placed, totally and fundamentally, in jeopardy. At the open grave or upon your own deathbed, you are inescapably exposed to the ultimate question: Is there anything final, conclusive? Here there is no longer any room for incomplete solutions. With many things you can live meaningfully; but can you also die with them meaningfully? You are constantly aware of the fact that nothing is given to you, either people or other creatures or experiences, that will always be with you and can make you wholly happy. Is death, then, the irrevocable end in which even the meaning of your life will be once and for all buried? Is there something that still sustains even when death has shattered everything? Is there some meaning which embraces life as a totality even over and beyond the grave? All answers lead into a dead-end street so long as they lack the dimension of the infinite.

0.3.7 The question of meaning and the question of faith. And thus, ultimately, the question of the final meaning of life inevitably leads into the question of God and turns into a question of faith. Consciously or unconsciously, you are looking for God. This primordial longing can be made to shift or it can be overpowered. But there simply is no full and true substitute for God. You cannot get away from God.

The psychologists have discovered a truly remarkable law. Genuine needs, which a person has suppressed, are always compensated for in some way. For example, by eating too much, by ostentatious living, and so on. The art of the psychotherapist consists in aiding his patient to discover this "other hunger" that is concealed beneath the physical or spiritual hunger. For many people, this "other hunger" is simply the suppressed longing for God, the final goal and meaning of our life.

Meaning is always involved with way and purpose and goal. The French language uses one and the same word for "meaning of life" and "reaching one's goal." And the German word for "meaning" comes from a stem that means something equivalent to "going in a direction towards a goal." Surely this is significant. When people are climbing a mountain, it is the peak itself that gives meaning to every step and to all the mighty effort. It is the goal which is always decisive. How could it be any different in our own path through life?

In the last analysis, man's eternal quest for meaning is a search for God. One of the greatest thinkers of all times has clothed his own personal experience of this constant unrest in these famous words: "You have made us for yourself, O God, and our heart is restless until it rests in you" (Augustine). The reflections we have just examined have once again borne out the truth behind the title of this book: Faith is Friendship!

Faith Is Friendship

PART ONE:

CHRISTIAN FAITH IS FAITH IN A PERSON

1. KNOWING GOD: IN AND WITH THE HEART (FAMILIARITY WITH GOD)

1.0 Faith is Friendship: "In the name of Christ I beg you: accept the friendship that God offers to you" (2 Cor 5:20).

> The word is near to you. It is in your mouth and in your heart. The word of faith that we preach. Thus if you confess Jesus as Lord with your mouth and believe in your heart that God has awakened him from the dead, you will be redeemed. For with the heart we believe, and this leads to justice; and with the mouth we confess, and this leads to salvation (Rm 10:8-10).

1.1 Credo: I give my heart

Credo! To us Christians this Latin word is intimate and familiar more than any other: it is a word we love. This little word begins our confession of faith, the essential cataloguing of what we believe.

Credo! In English: *I believe*. The Christian Gospel is a proclamation which strikes me very personally. And I am unique. I have a name. "I have called you by name. You are mine" (Is 43:1). Believing means giving an answer. I believe in you. I let my whole, entire self go out to you. You become the one real center about which my faith and my life revolve, for you can be ultimately relied upon and trusted in. Since believing is such an entirely personal affair, the first part of this book has been written partially in the first person. I am every man who believes, the Everyman of Faith.

Credo. On the basis of its original Latin, we should be translating this word as "I give my heart." To you, God, I make a present of my heart; in you I set my whole trust. Faith thus begins in my heart, in the very core of my being. It is a personal experience in my innermost self, a loving surrender and a lasting bond with the Person of God. That is why Christian faith is so alive, so total, and so incomprehensible. In the last analysis, it quite eludes the grasp of understanding and of psychology. Faith can be just as deep an experience and, at the same time, just as simple as is the experience of two people who are in love. And at the same time, one can never sufficiently stress the fact that the light of faith always has something of the darkness of faith mixed in with it.

1.2 Believing in a thing

1.2.0 What is Christian faith? What is the decisive and distinguishing Christian element about it?

1.2.1 The accidentals of faith. For many people the answer, unfortunately, sounds something like this: Christian faith is a sum of truths of faith which we have to accept; doctrines which we have to know; a teaching which attempts to explain our world and to resolve the riddles of human existence. It is a collection of unpleasant demands and obligations, of commandments and prohibitions; a defective knowledge of God and the things of the hereafter which we cannot understand; forms of divine service and formulas of prayer. There could hardly be any cruder way to delineate the reality of Christian faith. The good news of Christ does not consist primarily in curbs and checks and precepts; in forms and formulations; in a thousand and one non-essentials. This is what I call the accidentals of faith. A person could grow tired of such a faith very quickly.

1.2.2 Faith as doing. The pious men of the Old Testament made every effort to preserve the 365 prohibitions and the 248 precepts of the Law. If a man followed that Law he considered himself to be just in the presence of God. Then comes Jesus. He does not come in any way to take away the Law and the Prophets (Mt 5:17). Quite the contrary. He himself makes demands that sound hard and almost inhuman. His disciples are to leave everything, deny themselves, follow after him, and if need be proclaim their faith in him by giving up their own lives. But, in his turn, Jesus calls the whole rationale of this activity into question. The commandments are not a purpose unto themselves. They are a means to an end. They are supposed to show me the way to God. Behind the commandments stand God the loving Father, and the Redeemer Jesus Christ. All the precepts of Christianity radiate from the fundamental commandment which begins with these words: "You shall love the Lord your God with your whole heart" (Mt 22:37; Mk 12:30; Lk 10:27), and from the commandment of our Lord: "I give you a new commandment: Love one another, as I have loved you" (Jn 15:12). The decisive element in this new approach is the total orientation towards another Person.

1.2.3 Faith as knowing. It is also true, and important too, that believing is knowing. This means an agreement to truths and doctrinal formulas of belief. Who could deny it? Believing certainly means holding to a teaching as true, but doesn't mean losing oneself in a bewildering multitude of details. Not all tenets of our faith have the same rank and value. There is a definite rank and precedence among the articles of faith (Vatican II: *Decree on Ecumenism*, No. 11).

Christ himself has unmistakably pronounced this truth. The absolute center of all the articles of faith is a Person: "I am the truth" (Jn 14:6). In the totality of the Person of Jesus Christ are concentrated all the truths of faith. And thus I believe not in my own assertions about God, but in HIM. "Believe in God . . . and believe in me" (Jn 14:1). In believing I thus give assent, in the last analysis, not to truths which have been revealed to me or in favors which have been presented to me. Rather, I am saying Yes to a Person, a You, who has revealed this truth to me or made a present of this good deed to me. Around this one central point—Jesus Christ— turns all of Christian believing. "I know whom I have believed" (2 Tm 1:12).

1.3 Faith in a Person

1.3.0 Believing as a Christian thus means that I commit myself wholly to the loving person of God who has revealed himself in his Son Jesus Christ; that I make him my own security; that I base my entire existence upon him; that I am privileged to experience the happiness of his presence in a trustful sense of surrender. Faith as knowledge and faith as experience, believing a fact and believing a person, are not mutually exclusive activities. They complement each other. Otherwise faith and believing would inevitably result in a breach of equilibrium. Faith is friendship.

1.3.1 The partner, God. The happiest message to be found in the entire Bible is the message that our God is neither simply a Being of a higher order, nor merely an impersonal something or other. He is the personally loving Being who understands me and in whose presence I can learn to take refuge. In Scripture, it is true, he is often described as the Unapproachable, the Incomprehensible, the Unfathomable, the Wholly Other. (A God who could be comprehended in terms of human understanding would no longer be a god at all!) But there is quite a different picture of God painted in much brighter colors elsewhere in the Bible. God is presented as Father (Ho 11:1-4; Mt 7:11; Lk 15:11-32; 1 Jn 3:1), as Friend (Gn 12:1-3, 18:17-33; Ex 33:11; Jn 15:15), as Bridegroom (Ho 2:18; Is 54:4-10; Sg (entire book); Ep 5:25-27), yes, even as Mother (Is 66:13; Ho 11:1-8; Ps 139:5). He has a countenance. This implies something present, close. God is wholly in our presence. He turns his face to me. He has a heart that is beating for me. He "has to have mercy on me" (Jr 31:20), and he cannot do otherwise (Ho 11:8). Indeed, the Bible does not shrink from speaking of God's feelings. It is particularly some books of the Old Testament that describe the "feelings of God" in a very drastic manner, all too human for our modern conception of things, so that some of these descriptions have a way of turning us off today.

1.3.2 The partner, Man. Friendship means joining your heart to someone in partnership. I have been created as the image and partner of God. I can look for God and find him; I can experience both his grandeur and his love; perceive his voice and experience his presence. I can recognize him in faith. As a small child, I was declared a Christian without being asked. Certainly I was already deeply affected by Christ. But I do not become totally a Christian until I personally accept the proffered friendship and surrender myself to him in a personal decision.

1.3.3 Believing in friendship. Friendship between God and man: that is Christian faith. "We believe with the heart" (cf. Rm 10:9-10). "I call you friends" (Jn 15:15). But the heart does not use a bridle on its love: it does not set any bounds or limits. "May Christ dwell in your hearts in faith. May you be rooted and firmly founded in love. Then you will be able to grasp fully, with all the holy ones, the breadth and length and height and depth of Christ's love, and experience this love which surpasses all knowledge" (Ep 3:17-19). Faith means daring to enter into this enchanted circle of love; to make my way into this space of love which God has opened; to find my home there; to cling to the Lord with my heart, where the ultimate decisions take place. "We belong to the Lord in life and in death" (Rm 14:8).

Faith experienced in this manner can influence my life through and through. It elevates me decisively above the level of merely believing in a thing, the normal attitude of faith. Faith is, after all, neither a complicated structure of thought (even on the subject of God) nor the acceptance of a world-view or philosophy, but fidelity to the loving person of God. This faith is just as difficult to describe as it is radically simple to live. Bride and bridegroom, mother and child encounter each other without their I—you relationship being subjected to a long series of scientifically reasoned analysis. This is the way it has to be in my relationship with God as well.

1.4 Faith as invitation and encounter

1.4.0 Friendship cannot be forced. In the same manner, a person cannot "make" faith or be forced into faith. "A man is forced to live and a man is forced to die, and between these two points he is bound in almost everything he does. Only in the case of God is nobody ever forced. In this area God has made the human soul completely free" (Gertrud von Le Fort).

1.4.1 Knock. God does not force himself upon me. He draws me to himself. How often the Gospel records words of invitation: "Come to me all you who are weary and are heavy burdened" (Mt 11:28). "Follow me" (Mt 4:14, 9:9). "Listen well. Here I stand, knocking at the door. If anyone hears me calling and opens the door, I will enter his house and have supper with him, and he with me" (Rv 3:20). Christian faith means being open towards God and freely acceding to his invitation. This requires a good deal of humility. When all is said and done, there is only one type of person who is simply incapable of being given a present: the satiated, who needs no one and no thing. Without this interior preparedness on my part, God cannot give me any gift at all. He never overpowers, but only gives an invitation.

1.4.2 It is the Lord. Faith is anything but a theoretical assent to dry catechism formulas. Faith proceeds from encounter, and thus it is essentially experience. St. John described that fact at the very beginning of his first letter:

> This is what we proclaim to you: what was from the beginning, what we have heard, what we have seen with our eyes, what we have looked upon and our hands have touched—we speak of the word of life. (This life became visible; we have seen and bear witness to it, and we proclaim to you the eternal life that was present to the

Father and became visible to us). What we have seen and heard we proclaim in turn to you so that you may share life with us. This fellowship of ours is with the Father and with his Son, Jesus Christ. Indeed, our purpose in writing you this is that our joy may be complete (1 Jn 1:1-4).

Another important element of faith is a man's sense of being deeply stirred, and his self-surrender as an answer. In the New Testament the authors describe, each in his own way, their personal experience of Christ (Ph 2:6-11, 3:8-21; Rm 8:28-39; Heb 1:1-4; 1 Jn 1:1-4, 4:7-21; 1 P 1:3-5, 16-21). Some of them do so with a passion that appears very strange. St. Paul, for example, writes this in the overflowing enthusiasm of his heart:

> I have come to rate all as loss in the light of the surpassing knowledge of my Lord Jesus Christ. For his sake I have forfeited everything; I have accounted all else rubbish so that Christ may be my wealth and I may be in him, not having any justice of my own. . . . The justice I possess . . . has its origin in God and is based on faith (Ph 3:8-9).

After Easter the disciples had to learn to know Jesus all over again. "We no longer look on anyone in terms of mere human judgment. If at one time we so regarded Christ, we no longer know him by this standard" (2 Cor 5:16). They had to come to a renewed sense of faith; they had to take up the challenge of following the Risen Savior. "It is the Lord" (Jn 20:18, 25). Jesus is alive: that was the greatest surprise for the Apostles. Thomas is privileged to touch the Risen Savior and put his hands into the wound in Christ's side. He wants to know, with his own senses, if this is truly the Crucified Savior. After this contact with Christ, Thomas confesses his faith: "My Lord and my God." But Jesus stresses the primacy of faith over seeing: "Blest are they who have not seen and have believed" (Jn 20:24-29).

1.5 Faith as gift and promise

1.5.0 Thus Christian believing is never primarily an accomplishment of the human person, something he might be able to imagine or work out for himself. Faith is first of all and fundamentally an invitation, an encounter, a friendship, and thus a gift of grace.

1.5.1 The surprises of faith. I believe! That means that I cling to Jesus of Nazareth, the Christ. I put my trust in him. I open my heart to him, and give him free access to all my world. This encounter makes a claim upon my entire person—not only my knowledge, my understanding and my will, but my "heart." Such an experience of the heart is not without its precious gifts, such as trust and hope, consolation and joy, freedom and redemption. "Your faith has made you whole" (Mk 10:52).

1.5.2 No heart can imagine. The happiness of believing is always the promise. It elicits longing. "O God, you are my God whom I seek: for you my flesh pines and my soul thirsts like the earth, parched, lifeless and without water" (Ps 63:1). Human love, too, leads above and beyond itself; it is promise and hope. As a believer I love, above and beyond what I know, the unknown that I can only imagine. "We are all pilgrims. He alone is a Christian who realizes that despite his house and home he is always on the way" (Augustine). Here below, the eternal home and the eternal sense of being with the Lord are things we can only grasp by faith (1 Th 4:17). At every encounter with Christ I hurl myself forward in eager anticipation to reach this goal, for "Eye has not seen, ear has not heard, nor has it so much as dawned on man what God has prepared for those who love him" (1 Cor 2:9). "God is greater than our hearts" (1 Jn 3:20). This unheard-of promise has become my home and source of happiness.

1.5.3 Help my lack of faith. If faith lives upon promise and hope, believing is also always a step into the unknown, into the darkness and folly of the Gospel. Nothing could be more mistaken than to suppose that believing is a state of constant enthusiasm and high spirits, a feeling of happiness that lasts and lasts. The man who loves is intensely involved with his beloved. But even the most ideal partners can neither wholly grasp nor wholly possess each other. Quite the contrary. Friendship is a constantly renewed seeking after the beloved, a state of being on one's way towards the other. Always the one remains to some extent a mystery to the other, a mystery that can be imagined but never totally grasped.

But now, in faith, I approach the Incomprehensible: "Do not touch me" (Jn 20:17). I meet with the Wholly Other: "God is God and not a man" (Ho 11:9; Rm 11:33-36). The Old Testament already declares over and over again that faith is called to account and that it can grow in crisis. The prayer of the man in the Gospel expresses this tension inherent in faith, in clear and open words: "Lord, I believe; help my lack of faith" (Mk 9:24). Even the greatest saints speak of their interior dryness, of an

agonizing experience with God in which they have the feeling that God has abandoned them. They felt that they had become seekers after a God who was "hiding somewhere behind them."

1.6 Faith as "acquaintance" with God

Put simply, Christian believing is friendship, and at the same time is an "acquaintance" with God. Acquaintance implies knowledge. It implies at once both a knowledge of the heart directed towards the person loved (knowing the person), and a constantly renewed experience of a loving relationship with that person (understanding the person). It also implies a blessed experience of joy and gratitude (appreciating the person), and an enthusiastic willingness to declare oneself for him or her (acknowledging the person). I make myself "recognized, known" to God in my heart. This process of making myself recognized and familiar to God is like an acquaintanceship with him. But it is an acquaintance in faith, for every knowledge of God here below can only be a knowledge of faith.

2. KNOWING GOD: KNOWING WHO HE IS (IMAGE OF GOD)

2.0 God, who are you? From time immemorial, men have come before God in their searching with this same question: God, who are you?

God indeed remains the same, yesterday and today. But man's images of God and his experiences of God can change over the course of time. So it was in the various epochs of Israel's history. And so it is in the various stages of an individual human life.

2.1 Divine revelation

God I can neither grasp nor understand; neither analyze within my mind nor compute with electronic machines; neither prove beyond all objections by my reason nor seize with my five senses. I can meet with him if he himself takes the initiative in coming to meet me, if he appears to me and reveals himself to me. Now God actually has revealed himself, over and over again. That is why we call him the God of revelation and history.

2.1.1 "God is near to us" (Dt 4:7). The Gospel recounts the encounter between this man-seeking God and this God-seeking man. In other religions it is man who takes the first step in the search for God, but in

Christianity it is God who comes to man first, in order to reveal and proclaim himself. Our God does not speak from a distance, or from on high, into his world. Rather he expresses himself by taking hold of human history, by communicating himself. In Christ, in an incomparable manner, God seeks out a way to be close. Mother and child, bride and bridegroom, husband and wife mutually know each other and reveal themselves to each other when they share their love and closeness. In Christ, God himself is close to us. Out of love he has given himself to us: "And the Word was made flesh and dwelt among us" (Jn 1:14).

2.1.2 "The Lord, the God of Israel" (Is 45:3). Israel did not find its God by itself, or reason out his existence by itself. It encountered Yahweh in the events of its history: at its choosing, at the wandering through the desert, in its encounter with God on Mount Sinai, in the Promised Land. Israel interpreted these experiences correctly: God had revealed himself; God had shown us how much he loves us. In their gratitude, the Israelites were amazed that their people were so dear to Yahweh.

These experiences with God were faithfully interpreted, recounted, passed down, and then collected and recorded in the books of the Old Testament. Every generation saw something similar in the eyes of faith: "I had heard of you by word of mouth, but now my eye has seen you" (Jb 42:5).

The people of many generations and centuries have tried to clothe their experiences with God in words, and to delineate the countenance of the God who revealed himself to them.

Yahweh's activity in the history of Israel before the birth of Christ, together with the word of God in the Old Testament, constitutes what we call the "revelation of God in the Old Covenant." In Israel, faith in God rests upon this revelation experience. That is why, for Israel, God is not only God, but "the God of Israel," "God who has done great deeds," "our God."

In the New Covenant as well, Christian faith can be reduced to divine revelation in Christ, and the experience of God in him. We call the Risen Savior "our Lord," because in the two thousand years since the birth of Christ so many men have met him in faith, and experienced his loving closeness. My own individual experience is solidly rooted in the history of other people's experience too.

2.2 The experience of God

2.2.0 We are living in a sober, technical world. For many people, the only reality is what they can grasp and measure, what they can experience

with their senses. To a large degree there is a gap between what they experience and what they believe. Must we not, today more than ever before, point up faith as experience of God? What a deep-seated and powerful experience it is, at once the source of happiness and pain.

I need only open the Bible, the book which recounts the history of God with mankind. There I meet, over and over again, God, on the one hand, who loves men without bounds, and on the other hand, man, who is longing for the closeness of God. As soon as God appears to man, he is made happy, and yet he still experiences the closeness of God as something painful. Indeed, he cannot bear this closeness. Without comprehension, man stands before the presence of God. He suddenly realizes that man can never "possess" God. Even the people of God are not permitted simply to dispose of God. For God is precisely the Wholly Other: "But my face you cannot see, for no man sees me and still lives" (Ex 33:20). Encounter with God always means at once closeness and distance, understanding and incomprehension, wonder and astonishment, security and anxiety, love and fright, intimacy and reverence. This painful and happy experience very frequently involves the upheaval of our entire human existence.

2.2.1 In the Old Testament.
    4ADAM. Our first parents hid themselves from God's face. The Lord called out: "Adam, where are you?" He answered: "As soon as I heard the sound of your steps in the garden, I was afraid" (Gn 3:8-10).
    ABRAHAM. One day the Lord spoke to Abraham: "Set forth out of your land and away from your relations and out of the house of your father." So Abraham set forth as the Lord had commanded him (Gn 12:1-4). God put Abraham to the test and said to him: "Take your son Isaac, your only one, whom you love, . . . and offer him up as a holocaust on the height I will point out to you" (Gn 22:1-14).
    MOSES. From the thornbush God called to him: "Moses, Moses." He answered: "Here I am." Then God ordered him: "Do not come any closer. Take off your shoes. For the place where you are standing is holy ground." Then Moses covered his face, for he was afraid to look upon God (Ex 3:4-6).
    THE PROPHETS. "Woe is me, I am doomed! For I am a man of unclean lips, living among a people of unclean lips; yet my eyes have seen the King, the Lord of hosts" (Is 6:5).

2.2.2 In the Incarnation. In the Incarnation, God breaks with this painful element of the experience. The unapproachable God appears in the form of a child, who is not a threat to anyone. He lies there defenseless and helpless in his crib. From his mother he begs for love and care. "The cry of one birth has shattered the idols" (Kurt Marti). This God-made-Man is so full of human friendliness. "The kindness and love of God our Savior appeared" (Tt 3:4). In this Word made Flesh, God is so infinitely distant and yet so close, so incomprehensibly other and still so similar to all of us. God and Man. God-Man!

2.2.3 In the Eucharist. Here I no longer need to meet my God in fear and trembling. Here the encounter with God is anything but a painful experience. The All-powerful God comes to me as my brother, as my nourishment, as bread for which I hunger.

2.2.4 In faith and love. In the last analysis, I can grasp God only in faith and with the heart. Even as a believer, I suffer my whole life long for God. Something similar happens in the case of other people. When I love someone, I can never get enough of them. Their image constantly changes within me. "Love sets us free from every likeness" (Max Frisch). Like nothing else, friendship knows how to grasp much that is incomprehensible. The man who loves, sees and understands more. Love and knowledge mutually help each other to grow. Faith is friendship. Doesn't this mean that love of God, experience of God, and image of God are most intimately related? "He who obeys the commandments he has from me is the man who loves me; and he who loves me will be loved by my Father. I too will love him and reveal myself to him" (Jn 14:21).

2.3 The image of God

2.3.0 Would I like to be God? Would I like to be just as I present God to myself? The all-decisive question is not whether I believe in "something" or in a God, but rather in what God I believe. Who is my God for me? What "countenance" does my God have? What is the image of God I carry around with me?

2.3.1 Image of God as symbol. My image of God? Here I must guard against some very finely camouflaged temptations. I dare not ever debase my image of God into a sort of self-image. If I simply project my good experiences with others, or project the best of myself into the infinite and then extrapolate it into my image of God, what I thus create is not God at all. It is only my mirror image polished up, an ennobled double of myself, a projection of my own experiences. There is a further danger, which can be even more insidious. I might attempt to grasp God simply as an image, in human concepts and ways of expression. I attempt to reduce God, "whom the heavens cannot grasp" (1 K 8:27), into a mere image. This God would no longer be a God, but only a cheap substitute: a self-made idol. It was for this reason that God, in the Old Testament, forbade the Israelites to make any graven images of him (Ex 20:4-5).

Every image of God can, finally, only be a symbol. That is, an indication of something beyond our grasp, a passage through to the incomprehensible, a pale representation of something wholly different, an indistinct reminiscence of him, a more or less successful union with the Person of God.

2.3.2 The image reveals and conceals God. God is not a riddle, such as I might hope to ever solve. He remains a mystery. It is true that God reveals himself to me, and that I can meet him in faith. And still I will never succeed in recognizing him completely. Even the most intimate friends of Christ and God can only stammer contradictions. For example, John the Beloved Disciple writes on the one hand: "We have heard. . . . We have seen with our own eyes. Our hands have touched" (1 Jn 1:1). And on the other hand: "No man has ever seen God" (Jn 1:18; 1 Jn 4:12). "His voice you have never heard, his form you have never seen" (Jn 5:37). Or St. Paul, the Apostle to the Gentiles: "No human being has ever seen or can see" (1 Tm 6:16). And on the other hand: "The kindness and love of God our Savior appeared" (Tt 3:4). "God is truly among you" (1 Cor 14:25).

Only God himself can reveal an image of God to me. But the image can always conceal or obscure him completely. For God surpasses every human conception. Even when I capture him in an image, he immediately slips away.

2.3.3 Every image of God is surpassable. My image of God can never, accordingly, embrace him in his totality. And thus I must always distinguish between God and the image that I make of God for myself.

My experience of God forms the living backdrop for my image and conception of him. There are no "fixed" images of God, because there is a constant correspondence between the image of God and the experience of God. The two mutually influence each other. New experiences of God will alter my image of God, and a new image of God will leave its stamp upon the life of my faith. Since the image of God is changeable, it can mature or degenerate. One decisive goal of the pastoral care of souls, of preaching and Christian upbringing, must be to cooperate in the formation of a mature and genuine image of God. Disfigured images of

God must be corrected and false ones shattered. God as artisan, God as rival of humanity, God as fellow traveler and handyman for humanity, as grand superintendent, as a bank or supermarket for grace, as a makeshift or the fulfillment of a wish or an all-round insurance—all of these are false images, caricatures of God.

My image of God and my life must not be in contradiction with each other. That would lead to serious difficulties in faith.

When I reject an outmoded image or false conception of God, I do not hereby necessarily lose God himself, but only a caricature of God. It would be destructive only if I were to abjure my false conceptions of God without at the same time trying to achieve a more genuine image of God.

2.4 Talking about God

2.4.0 God is infinitely exalted. In speaking about him the power of human speech can only fail. In any event, I must never create the impression that I know anything about God based on my own resources.

2.4.1 *"You shall not take the name of God in vain" (Lv 19:12)*. Out of pure reverence for the Wholly Other, the Israelites never dared to even pronounce the name of God. In the course of history this same name has been used and misused for and against every conceivable purpose. Martin Buber writes that

> God is the most loaded word of all human words. No other word has been so soiled, so mangled. Generations of mankind have brought to bear the entire weight and burden of their anxiety-ridden life against this word and brought it to the ground: it lies in the dust and is made to support their whole burden. The generations of mankind with their religious splinter-groups have torn the word to shreds. They have killed for it and they have died for it. It bears all their fingerprints and all their blood. They draw up caricatures and write God's name upon them: they murder each other and say it is in the name of God. We cannot wash the word "God" clean, and we cannot make it whole; but we can lift it from the dirt, sullied and soiled though it be.

2.4.2 *Stammering about God*. Even when I speak about God, I am forced to fall back upon human words and human conceptions. Even the writers of the Bible speak of God's "countenance" and "voice," of his "hands" and "finger" and "eyes." This human manner of speaking about God is certainly not incorrect. But it is destined always to remain an awkward stammering.

God, who are you? On the subject of God I can speak in more than one way; that is to be expected. But I must always do so with great reserve. For I can never wholly grasp him in terms of human concepts. God himself says: "I am God and not a man" (Ho 11:9). As a result, I shall not attempt to paint a "tasteful" picture of God with learned theories and deliberations. Rather, I shall address the problem simply and directly. God, what do you say about yourself? How does the Bible describe you?

2.5 The personal God

God, as Scripture describes him, is not a "higher being," nor a "superior power," nor an "all-embracing It," but rather a "You" and an "I."

In every color and variation and image and comparison, the Bible represents him as Someone, as a Person: as King (Ezk 20:33; Is 52:7) and Shepherd (Ezk 34; Mi 4:6; Zp 3:19), as Father (Ho 11:1-9; Jr 31:15-20; Is 64:7; Ml 2:10; Mt 6:6-15, 10-20; Lk 10:21-22, 15:11-32; Jn 5:18) and Mother (Is 66:13; Ho 11:1-4; Ps 139:5), as Friend and loving Partner (Sg; Jn 15:14; 2 Cor 5:20), One who meets with man and calls him by name: "I call you by your name; you are mine" (Is 43:1).

God calls me by name. My name? That is what I am, and that is my whole history. And what does it mean when a Lover calls his beloved by name? Doesn't that mean: "You know me, and you know about me, and you accept me; in your presence I can simply be my own self"? Christian faith is a personal faith, a faith that is directed towards a person. "Believe in God and believe in me" (Jn 14:1).

2.6 The living God

When I think of wars and murders, acts of terror and abortions, I might come to believe that life today had lost its value. And still I cling to life with every fiber of my being. I rejoice in life, I am in love with it, and I am all but intoxicated with it. That is why only a living God can stir me to enthusiasm. Only for him is it worth my while to dedicate my entire life. For a dead being, no one would give up his own life.

2.6.1 "God of Life (Mk 12:27). By way of contrast to the dead idols, our God is "not a God of death, but a God of life" (Mk 12:27). He gives himself these names: "God of life, the living God" (Ps 42:3; 1 S 19:6). In Israel people swore not by the "true God," but by the "living God" (Is 14:39, 45; 2 S 4:9, 12:5, 14:11). When God himself wants to stress a statement with particular emphasis, he swears "by his own life" or "as truly as I live" (Nb 14:21, 28; Jr 22:24; Ezk 5:11) or "as truly as I live for eternity" (Dt 32:40).

2.6.2 "Friend of life" (Ws 11:26). He calls to life, and thus presents himself as the fountainhead of life, in that he has created all living beings and the living human person out of nothing (Gn 1:20-27, 2:7; Ws 15:11). This same God wants his creatures to be fruitful, to multiply and to pass on the gift of life (Gn 1:22, 28). As "Friend of life" (Ws 11:26) he has "no joy in the destruction of life" (Ws 1:13; Ezk 18:32; Ps 104:29-30). That is why he wants "the sinner to be converted to live forever" (Ezk 18:32, 33:11). In fact, he even protects life with an individual commandment of its own: "You shall not kill" (Ex 20:13; Gn 9:5).

2.6.3 "I am the Life" (Jn 11:25). In the fullness of time Jesus came into this world, "so that we would have life and have it abundantly" (Jn 10:10). "The Father has granted it to the Son to have life in himself" (Jn 5:26). The disciples offer their testimony: "You are the Son of the Living God" (Mt 16:16). Christ says of himself that he is "the resurrection and the life" (Jn 11:25, 14:6). It is true that he lays down his life (Jn 10:11, 15, 17; 1 Jn 3:16), but then he is victorious over death (1 Cor 15:54-57; Rm 6:8) and "takes up his life again" (Jn 10:17-18). To his friends the Risen Savior says: "I am the Living One. I was dead. But behold, I live for eternity" (Rv 1:18). This fact fills his disciples with joy and enthusiasm: Alleluia! Christ lives! (Lk 24:41, 52).

2.6.4 "Author of Life" (Ac 3:15). Christ, the Redeemer, becomes the "Prince and Author of life" (Ac 3:15). "If we died with Christ, we believe that we are also to live with him" (Rm 6:8) "For me, 'life' means Christ" (Ph 1:21). Thus I can say: "The life I live now is not my own; Christ is living in me" (Gal 2:20). For now it is still true that "our life is hidden now with Christ in God" (Col 3:3). It demands faith of us for now. "Whoever believes in me will never die" (Jn 3:16, 11:26). But one day, "When Christ our life appears, then you shall appear with him in glory" (Col 3:4). Then there will be no more death (Rv 21:4). There will be life for all. Can such a friend of life fail to stir our enthusiasm?

2.7 The loving God

2.7.0 Life is committed to love: "God is love. God's love was revealed in our midst in this way: He sent his only Son to the world that we might have life through him. Love, then, consists in this: not that we have loved God but that he has loved us and has sent his Son as an offering for our sins" (1 Jn 4:8-10).

2.7.1 The "dear" God. Love today is a much over-used word. It has a thousand and one meanings. But without love, no one can live. When a man goes out from his own loneliness to encounter a loving other, and when the two of them find each other in the happiness of their love, then he sees everything with different eyes: himself, the world, his fellow man. Indeed, then he will even acquire some presentiment of the love of God.

But on the other hand, it can be deadly, and life can be without meaning if, instead of loving acceptance, a man encounters nothing but cruelty. Today it is precisely the suffering in the world that troubles so many people. In Auschwitz or other concentration camps they saw God cruelly dying in human beings. Any talk about a dear or loving God and his boundless good will towards man is considered by many as impudent derision or pious lies.

> A people who have offered up two million dead can perhaps have the right to ask God what he was thinking about. But if God does not answer, not for these two million; and not for the millions that people have killed before this; and not for the children either that lie along the streets and roads starving and crippled; when he not only will not answer but even actually looks as though he would not answer any more readily for twenty or thirty millions, a silent God, cold in his indifference, . . . then it could be that here and there it might be too much for someone to kneel before the stone wall and get only an echo for an answer. It might be that he will ask himself what kind of a love that is, if it consists only in sacrifices and silence. If it lets blood flow day and night, streams of blood; if it lets all the victims groan, day and night, victims of every age, good and bad, guilty and innocent alike. And just sits there in silence and decides that it has done well. (Ernst Wiechert)

Now obviously it is very wrong to conclude that God should be held responsible for all the sorrow and suffering in the world. And still the problem of suffering in the world remains an inexorable and constant question before God. I too have to be concerned about the problem.

2.7.2 "God is love" (1 Jn 4:8). Every love has its story. The same is true of God's love for and with mankind. The entire Old Testament represents a God who acts out of love. God loves the way a friend loves his friend (Ex 33:11; Is 41:8); the way a vine-dresser loves his vineyard (Is 5:1-7; Ezk 17:1-10); the way a bridegroom loves his bride: "As a bridegroom rejoices in his bride, so shall your God rejoice in you" (Is 62:5). Or the way a mother loves her child: "As a mother comforts her son, so will I comfort you" (Is 66:13). "Can a mother forget her infant, be without tenderness for the child of her womb? Even should she forget, I will never forget you" (Is 49:15). "I have drawn you to me with bands of love" (Ho 11:4).

The books of the Old Testament describe the experiences of love that the people of Israel had with God: "The Lord, the Lord, a merciful and gracious God, slow to anger and rich in kindness and fidelity" (Ex 34:6). All these descriptions of the love of God climax finally in one very central and profoundly deep revelation: our God is "a God of love" (2 Cor 13:11); in fact God is love (1 Jn 4:8). Only a man who has had experience of God could speak like this. St. John does not say that God loves, but rather that God is love. Love is not only an attribute of God, but his very essence, his essential property. This marks the unheard-of originality and the unsurpassably unique character of Christianity.

2.7.3 "God so loved the world . . . " (Jn 3:16). "God's love was revealed in our midst in this way: he sent his only Son to the world that we might have life through him. Love, then, consists in this: not that we have loved God but that he has loved us and has sent his Son as an offering for our sins" (1 Jn 4:9-10). In Christ "the kindness and love of God our Savior appeared" (Tt 3:4). "We have known the love of God" (1 Jn 4:16). "He went about doing good" (Ac 10:38). And "He had loved his own in this world, and would show his love for them to the end" (Jn 13:1). This means that he loved them to the very end of his life, to his last breath, and also that he loved them in the most complete way, with absolute intensity. That was Christ's way of loving. "There is no greater love than this: to lay down one's life for one's friends" (Jn 15:13).

2.7.4 "He loved us first" (1 Jn 4:19). In an effort to describe God's love, Christ uses comparisons with human love: with the love of a father (Lk 11:11-13), of a friend (Jn 15:14), of a bridegroom (Mt 9:15), of brothers and sisters in a family (Mt 12:48-50). Christ also brought us the news that God loves like a God and not a man. He loves me even when there apparently is nothing lovable in me. His is an undeserved love, a love without meriting and without qualification. God's loving gift is in no way bound up with anything that I have to do first. He is compassionate and deeply concerned for the welfare of his people (Ex 3:7-10). He forgives and he saves. All this is implied in the wonderful statement that "he has loved us first" (1 Jn 4:19). That is why I can have such confidence. God my Father will not leave me in the lurch, especially since my heart is attached to God.

2.7.5 "Love comes from God" (1 Jn 4:7). This same God once said on the morning of creation: "Let us make man in our image, after our likeness" (Gn 1:26). God is love, and thus man is also an image of the love of God. The Bible goes still further when it states that "Our love comes from God" (1 Jn 4:7). "He who abides in love abides in God and God in him" (1 Jn 4:16). "The love of God has been poured out in our hearts through the Holy Spirit" (Rm 5:5). "See what love the Father has bestowed on us in letting us be called children of God! Yet that is what we are" (1 Jn 3:1). "His love endures for ever" (1 Ch 16:34).

2.8 God, coming and already nigh

2.8.0 "Where can I flee from your presence? If I go up to the heavens, you are there; if I sink to the nether world, you are there" (Ps 139:7-8). "God is not really far from any one of us" (Ac 17:27).

2.8.1 *"You are near, O Lord" (Ps 119:151)*. With God I, as a man, have the most contradictory experiences. Now I experience him as the distant and hidden God, the silent and withdrawing God. Then once again I am privileged to experience his closeness. He calls me by my name. Even when I do not see him, I still sense, in the darkness, his loving presence. Thus he is never unattainably distant, far away from me. Rather, he is the most intimate comrade, accompanying me along the way. He is in me. I find him in the innermost recesses of my heart. He hears me and knows me. He alone has the key to the ultimate source of my love, and has access to the deepest wellspring of my heart. With him I can speak, full of childlike trust.

2.8.2 *"I am Yahweh" (Ex 3:14)*. The Bible describes Paradise as a garden of delights, in which God and man dwell together, walk with each other for pleasure, and carry on a conversation. By his sin, man flees from the face of God and hides himself. God goes after him: "Adam, where are you?" (Gn 3:9). Since that time, man is in flight from God, and God is searching for him.

One day God reveals himself to Moses and the people of Israel as the close and brotherly God. Moses wants to know the name of the Lord. God answered: "I am Yahweh" (Ex 3:14). That means "I am there; I will be there." This name is the heart and core of all the good tidings of the Old Testament. The Lord is there in the history of mankind as "God with us and for us." This expression runs through the Bible like a refrain: "I am with you": with Abraham (Gn 12), Isaac (Gn 26:24), Jacob (Gn 28:15), Moses (Ex 33:11), Joshua (Jos 1:5), Gideon (Jg 6:16), Samuel (1 S 3:19), David (2 S 7:9), Hezekiah (2 K 18:7), Jeremiah (Jr 1:8, 19), and the entire people of Israel (Ps 46:8). The Israelites regard Yahweh as their liberator. They know that he has made a covenant with their forebears. Irrevocably he has bound himself to their people. Their whole destiny is bound up with him. They recognize the special signs of God's presence: the Holy City (Yahweh is there) (Ezk 48:35), the Temple and the Ark (Ezk 37:26; 1 K 8:10-13; 2 S 7:1-7). He is present in a cloud (Ex 40:34-38), in the fire (Ex 13:21-22, 24:17), in the storm (Ex 20:18). Yahweh is there in the history of mankind and helps to shape it (salvation history).

2.8.3 Emmanuel: God with us. God comes to man. In Jesus Christ, God is infinitely near as my brother. He has "appeared" (Tt 2:11) and become man. He has taken on human flesh and dwelt among us (Jn 1:14). His Name is Emmanuel, that is, "God with us" (Mt 1:23). In him God has, in the truest sense of the word, "a heart for us," even a human heart (Veneration of the Sacred Heart of Jesus). And he invites everyone to him: "Come to me, all you who are weary and find life burdensome, and I will refresh you" (Mt 11:28). Men meet with him. Over and over again in the New Testament we find expressions like this: "We have seen and heard him, looked upon him and touched him" (1 Jn 1:1; Jn 20:24-29; Lk 24:36-43). If these words are seen in the context of Christ and his salvation, there is a clear allusion to the experience of God's nearness.

Jesus Christ knows how close God is to man. He himself addresses God with the Jewish term of endearment "Abba" (Dear Father). For him God is not someone distant, but a trusted and loving Father. On the basis of this experience, Jesus proclaims the ever-new coming of God.

Especially after his Resurrection, Christ is near to us and is in our midst. "Where two or three are gathered in my name, there am I in their midst" (Mt 18:20). He is present in my life and bound to me. He dwells in me through faith (Ep 3:17), so that it is no longer "I who live, but Christ lives in me" (Gal 2:20). The man who believes in him becomes the dwelling of God (Ep 2:21-22), the temple of God (1 Cor 3:16-17, 6:19), the body of Christ (1 Cor 12:12-27). In the Eucharist he binds himself to me, for "the man who feeds on my flesh and drinks my blood remains in me, and I in him" (Jn 6:56). Emmanuel: God with us!

2.8.4 "We shall be with the Lord unceasingly" (1 Th 4:17). God is near to me, and at the same time is always the one destined to come. "Today you shall know that the Lord is coming and tomorrow you shall behold his glory" (Advent Liturgy). I hope to be someday "eternally with the Lord" (1 Th 4:17), "he with me and I with him" (Rv 3:20). "Then I shall see him face to face" (1 Cor 13:12).

3. KNOWING GOD: KNOWING WHAT HE DOES (THE MIGHTY DEEDS OF GOD)

3.1 The God I encounter in the Bible is not a relaxed and sleepy, idle and unworking God, but an active one. He reveals himself in manifold ways, but especially in events that mankind experiences as encounters with God. The Bible is not a theoretical treatise on the truths of God; it recounts his conduct and activity. God is at work "for us, for me." My faith, too, relies upon the activities of this divine Other. Believing means knowing what he has done for us, recognizing his wonderful works, and taking them seriously. "Your right hand has upheld me, and you have stooped to make me great" (Ps 18:36).

3.1 The wonderful works of God

God's love is inventive, and always full of surprises. He creates a splendid world and calls mankind into existence. Over and over again, he leaves his mark in human history, forgiving and saving. I am thinking of the liberation from the slavery of Egypt, the rescue at the Sea of Reeds, the revelation on Mount Sinai, the wonderful works during the wandering through the desert on the way to the Promised Land. .

When the fullness of time had come, God's Son became Man for us. Out of love for us, he died on the cross and arose from the dead. The name of Jesus means "Yahweh is salvation; liberator." This name is God's program for the world, for he does not capitulate in the face of evil. Through Christ, he wants to be present in the midst of the reality of our life, in order to redeem us. Jesus Christ is the climax and the all-conclusive focus of salvation history, and thus the focus of our faith. According to St. Paul, the death and resurrection of Christ is the greatest of God's wonderful works, and the true and proper subject of our faith: "If Christ was not raised, your faith is worthless" (1 Cor 15:17; cf. Col 2:12; Rm 8:11).

3.2 Creation

3.2.0 Part of modern man is tired of the world as it exists today; it nauseates him. But part of him is truly in love with creation; he passionately investigates the universe and its mysteries.

While we are learning to understand creation better, we should also arrive at a better knowledge of the Creator and a more profound appreciation of man's responsibility for what God intends. Manned space flights are fantastic achievements; but to date they have opened only a very small window onto the universe. But everything that we can see of the unending mystery of the universe through these windows confirms our certainty that there is a Creator (Wernher von Braun, rocket expert and pioneer of space exploration).

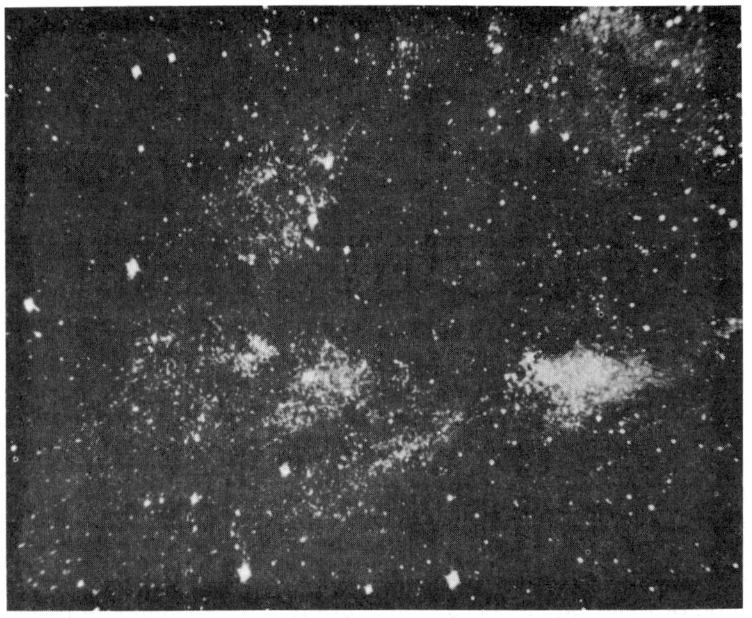

3.2.1 How big is your world. The world of the stars, the universe, all of creation can only awaken my sense of wonder.

The experts reckon the total number of galaxies (star systems after the manner of our Milky Way) in the universe at several hundred million.

The sun is a mighty ball of gas, 865,400 miles in diameter. In its interior there are temperatures of up to 36 million degrees Fahrenheit. In the sun, every second, some 660 million tons of hydrogen are transformed into helium.

The principal star in Auriga, epsilon, is two thousand times bigger than the sun.

With the naked eye we can see about five thousand stars. But in our Milky Way system alone there are more than one hundred million stars. Its diameter is approximately 100,000 light years.

In order to deal with these unimaginable distances, we speak of light years. By light year we understand the distance that light travels in the course of one year. Light hurtles along with an incredible velocity of 186,000 miles per second. That is, in one second it goes seven and one-half times around the earth.

The fixed star closest to our solar system is called Alpha Centauri. It is "only" 4.3 light years away from the sun. The following model might be of some help to understand the situation better. The distance between the earth and the sun is 93 million miles. If we reduce a million miles to a single foot, then the distance between earth and sun would be 93 feet and the distance between the sun and Alpha Centauri would be 1,136 miles.

In the constellation of Andromeda there is a famous spiral nebula. At a distance of 2.25 million light years, it is the most distant object that can be seen by the naked eye.

3.2.2 Amazement and questions. "Mighty and wonderful are your works, Lord God Almighty! . . . King of the nations!" (Rv 15:3). Francis of Assisi was aware of a deep fraternal bond with every living creature. His Canticle to the Sun is one of the most moving songs of praise for creation. A gardener brother once confided to me that he felt insulted every time people called the earth "dirt," because this so-called dirt was so mysterious and fruitful and holy. Whenever I climb a mountain, cross an ocean, or walk into a primeval forest, I am overcome by a feeling of infinity. I am seized with amazement at the colors of the sunset sky, at the sparkling of a drop of water, at the smile of the flowers. The wonderful world of the microscopic also holds me in its spell: the world of the atom and of radiation.

Then, once again I wonder at the deliberate balance and coordination of the powers of nature, the planned and orderly organization of living beings and their organs. The eye is designed for seeing. And yet it develops within the darkness of a mother's womb. Even though it does not as yet have any assigned function to fulfill, it is planned and prepared in advance: one day, it is destined to see!

On the other hand, there is much that is terrible and sinister in the world of nature. Plants wither, animals suffer or eat each other up. Storms leave behind them an inconsolable scene of devastation. Earthquakes, floods, avalanches and other natural catastrophes destroy so many people's homes.

When I contemplate the world, I begin to reflect and I ask myself: where does the world come from, with all its beauty and horror? Did it all originate as the result of blind chance, or was it planned in definite order? What is the meaning and purpose of the world? And how will it end?

3.2.3 Natural science and faith. The Bible is neither a scientific book nor the record of an eyewitness to the act of creation. It is not meant to research creation or to explain it. Bible and faith both tell us that God created the world. Just how the world came into being—that is the task of science to explain. Between natural science and faith there can be a contradiction only when the competences of the two provinces are overstepped.

3.2.4 The scientists interpret the world. The origins of the world go back hundreds of millions of years. This fact can be established by science beyond any objection. The precise age of the world, however, is not known. Everything depends upon what theory we settle on regarding the birth of the universe. The opinions of the experts differ considerably and fluctuate between five and fifteen billion years. Countless scientists have already done their research in an effort to determine how the world began. No one can give a sure answer. We are forced to fall back on hypotheses and theories.

One widely spread theory is the "big bang" theory. By way of broad generalization, this opinion of many experts is as follows:

According to this theory, millions of years ago, somewhere in the universe, an inconceivably vast quantity of matter was formed. This matter condensed and thereby became so hot that it exploded. The matter was shot out into the universe in glowing hot balls of gas. These bigger and smaller glowing gasballs moved with tremendous velocity from the source of the explosion. Many of them began to cool off, to condense once again into solid matter, and eventually formed the solar system with a sun in the center and the planets orbiting around it.

An incredible number of such solar systems form a milky way, a spiral nebula.

Our sun is still a glowing hot ball of gas. But our earth has cooled off some millions of years ago. At first the surface of the earth was still glowing hot. No life could form on it. All the water which today forms the seas was suspended in the air as water vapor. All the rain turned into steam as quickly as it began to fall. No ray of sunlight was able to penetrate this thick cloud of vapor. It was another few million years before the surface had cooled to the point that the molten matter grew solid and the rock formations began to form. The continents we know today developed like lumps on the surface of molten ocean. In the interior of the earth, this matter is still hot and molten (Günther Weber).

The oceans came into being. Life began and developed. The various species of plants and animals evolved and disappeared. Other species adapted themselves to the changing conditions of life. In an extremely complicated process of evolution, spreading over millions of years, the earliest anthropoids turned into man. Even today our world is not a finished product: it is destined to develop further. It is a world of changing and becoming.

Despite all this research, the really decisive questions are still unsolved riddles. How did all this get started in the beginning? What is the origin of the powers of nature that are so deliberately and orderly planned? Who brought this whole stupefying process into being?

3.2.5 The Bible interprets the world. Even the believer of the Old Testament could conclude directly from creation to the existence of a creator. The pious Israelites interpreted creation from the vantage point of their faith (Ps 95:3-5; Ps 148; Is 44:24). God created the world. He passed on the gift of his own life and love. That is why "your name, O Lord, is so glorious over all the earth" (Ps 8:10). Since he is "the creator of the heavens, who is God, the designer and maker of the earth who established it" (Is 45:18), the powers of nature must all obey him (Ps 114; Jb 26:7-14).

In the first book of the Bible there are two different creation narratives side by side. Gn 1:1-2:4a dates back from about 500 B.C. and is called the Priestly Tradition of creation. Gn 2:4a ff. dates from about 950 B.C. and is called the Yahwist tradition of creation. Neither of the two was intended to describe the external realities of creation. The author of the Priestly account, for example, portrays the origin of the world in the light of the current knowledge of the world. In the first three days, God creates three great areas: light and darkness, water, and land. Light and darkness are divided, and the area of light is established. The waters above the earth and below the firmament are separated, and the area of air is established. Land and sea are separated so that the area of the earth's surface is established. In the following three days these areas are furnished with an assortment of creatures. The sun, moon and stars are associated with the area of the light. Fish and birds inhabit the space that has been created by the separation of the waters. And on the surface of the earth there appear a series of land animals, and finally man.

The world picture of these ancient peoples does not correspond with the findings of modern science. But nonetheless already in the creation narrative there is a reference to a temporal development in different epochs (6 days). That is, a scale from the lower to the higher forms of life: plants, animals, man. At the end of this development stands man as king of creation (Gn 1:26-27). Created by God (Gn 2:7), he is on the one hand the partner of God, made in his own image (Gn 1:27), and on the other hand is related to all the rest of creation. Adam is taken from *adamah* ("the earth") (Gn 2:7). He receives from God the mandate to be lord over all the earth (Gn 1:26-28). Man takes part in creation, in that he has a responsibility to shape the future. "You have given man rule over the works of your hands, putting all things under his feet" (Ps 8:5-10).

The creation narrative closes with the remark that, on the seventh day, God saw all that he had created and it was very good (Gn 1:31). This indicates that the world and mankind, from the very beginning, exist in reference to God's mighty plans. He means to bind his creatures to himself in friendship. That is the scope of his plans. This friendship between God and man is characterized in the Bible as "Covenant." And this seventh day (the Sabbath in Jewish reckoning) is the great symbol of the covenant, the day of friendship.

In Christ, God has unexpectedly clarified his loving plans. He shows what he has in mind for mankind and for all his creation. "God so loved the world that he gave his only Son" (Jn 3:16). The New Testament puts an entirely new interpretation on the data of the creation narrative. Everything has been created in ultimate reference to Christ (Col 1:16). The development has not stopped even today. Christ is the goal and basis of creation (Heb 1:2-3). Creation is not dormant even now. "Creation groans and is in agony even until now" (Rm 8:22), "to be freed from its slavery to corruption and share in the glorious freedom of the children of God" (Rm 8:21). Only then, when the covenant of God is fully realized and Christ is all in all, will the word God spoke on the morning of creation be truly fulfilled in fact: "And God saw that it was very good" (Gn 1:31).

3.2.6 A poet interprets the world. Just as the personality of the artist shows through in a work of art, so the personality of God radiates throughout the innermost structure of all created things. All nature bears a stamp, a trademark of God. Everything bears the imprint of

God's fingers. There is a style about everything, the style of God; we can recognize that everything was created by the same artist.

Nature, too, is full of symbols which speak to us of God. All of creation is the calligraphy of God, and in this handwriting there is not a single character without its meaning. We are established in this creation, which is totally communication, as the purest and most beautiful of the words of God. We are God's image. This divine countenance is imprinted not only upon mankind, but upon all things of beauty.

All things love each other. The whole of nature is pressing towards a single You. All living creatures are bound up with one another. A mysterious power makes brothers of all plants and animals and things. All living things either love one another or feed on one another. They are all bound together in this all-embracing process of becoming and growing, propagating and dying. In nature everything is mutation and transformation. Everything is embracing, caressing, kissing. All things are in relationship to each other. One thing is understood only through another, and the other is understood through yet another, so that the whole universe is one single, all-embracing reality.

That is the rhythm of love. We are all bound up together and we are all incomplete. Nature herself, still incomplete, presses onward towards the highest perfection: this unconscious pressure is evolution.

In search for the creator, we turn to creatures—like the butterfly that dashes against the window pane. For creation is as transparent as glass, and the radiance of God shines through it.

All things speak of God, because all things sigh for God: the starry sky as well as the cricket too, the infinite galaxies and the striped squirrel that plays with everything and is afraid of everything and hides from everything.

All nature is in a flame of love, created by love in order to enkindle love in us. And my own body is created for love of God. Each individual cell in my body is a hymn to the Creator and an ever-present avowal of love.

The entire universe waits for its reunion with God from whom it proceeds. Away from God, all things are scattered and forced to seek union with other things. (Ernesto Cardenal)

3.3 The Incarnation

3.3.0 God becomes Man! Any attempt to speak about this results in helpless stammering. God is so other and so incomprehensible: over and over again, he is the source of constant surprise. But nothing has managed, in two thousand years, to set the world into such a state of amazement as the Incarnation, this irrevocable visit of God to his human creatures, this boldest adventure of love. The adventure of redemption began in a little house in Nazareth.

3.3.1 Genealogy of Jesus Christ (Mt 1:1). God becomes Man! The New Testament begins with the monotonous enumeration of names: "Abraham begot Isaac, Isaac begot Jacob, *etc.*" Apparently only a dry enumeration of names. But each of these names preserves a little bit of human and divine history, bringing it from the past into the present. One generation follows the other, in an endless series. Blood and life, love and guilt are passed on from one womb to another. And all of a sudden we catch our breath at what we see written before us: "Jacob was the father of Joseph, the husband of Mary. It was of her that Jesus who is called the Messiah was born" (Mt 1:16). The Gospel thus proclaims our Lord's roots in human history in the most solemn way possible: through a genealogy. God has made bold to enter into the history of mankind. He shares in it and helps to shape it.

3.3.2 Born of a woman (Gal 4:4). God becomes Man! The amazing thing is not that Jesus Christ is God, but that God became man in Jesus Christ. This reality of the Incarnation is so incomprehensible that it has kept men's minds occupied for two thousand years. There is a constant temptation to abbreviate this mystery of the faith: Jesus "played" at being either God or man. Even the early Church already had to come to terms, in a series of Councils, with this Jesus of Nazareth. Then the Church summed up her confession of faith in the simple and precise formula: Jesus Christ, true God and true Man. Son of God—Son of Man.

3.3.3 "The Word became flesh and made his dwelling among us" (Jn 1:14). Becoming man means becoming "brother." God's Son also became my brother, when he interwove himself into the fabric of our mortal flesh. "He emptied himself and took the form of a slave, being born in the likeness of men" (Ph 2:7). In his Incarnation God has delivered himself to me and established the highest degree of solidarity.

He shared our destiny. He allowed the whole burden of sinful humanity to be loaded upon himself and became the very incarnation of sin. In the Garden of Gethsemane he was helpless and confused and bore the misery of an over-burdened heart. On the way of the cross he was made a fool of, abused. On the cross he surrendered himself to the most bitter anxiety and meaninglessness and sense of final abandonment by God. His life here on earth ended in the agony of death and the darkness of the grave. Our Savior did not spare himself, and in his own self he experienced the drama of redemption. God is more human than we imagined. Jesus Christ, born into the human family, belongs to every person of every time. The Incarnation is not to be held back. It keeps happening, on and on, until the Lord comes again in glory. That is why Christmas is a focal point of salvation history: for the Incarnation substantiates and encompasses and evokes the death, Resurrection, and Second Coming of our Savior. With Christ, in Christ, time runs both backwards and forwards.

3.3.4 "They found the Child in the crib" (Lk 2:16). God becomes Man! God's kindness and friendship towards mankind has visibly appeared. That is why Christmas is called the festival of love. We bow down before the Child because he is so little, and before God because he is so great. In the presence of the Child in the crib we fall to our knees, because the great God has made himself so tiny out of love for us. God is subject to us men. In Christ, God has taken on a human face. The Child in the crib reveals to us the reality of the Incarnation, and at the same time the reality of God's gift to us: "God so loved the world that he gave his only Son" (Jn 3:16).

3.3.5 "I bring you news of great joy!" (Lk 2:10). God becomes Man! The history of the world is dark. It will continue to be written in blood and tears. But is it not destined to have a happy outcome, if God himself has once played a role in it and has written his Word into mankind and into the progression of time? Our earth is a swarm of disillusioned, embittered, despairing people. And yet it is still an enviable thing to be a human being, if God has shown such great love for man and his poor human flesh. Men can be vicious with each other. Hearts can be hard and unsympathetic. And still we must not despair of the human heart. God himself chose to use the human heart in order to love through it. Karl Rahner believes that since the Incarnation it is only proper to bear our Brother's kindness and friendship towards man in our own hearts. "God

himself has tried it with this heart of ours, and he has told us that it can
work. His experience is more decisive and believable than our own: we
can be better than we believe."

3.4 Jesus Christ the Redeemer

3.4.0 The eyewitnesses to the events in the life of Jesus of Nazareth
have long been dead. And still this same Jesus Christ leaves mankind no
rest, right down to our present day. Again and again, the words of St.
Peter prove true: "Although you have never seen him, you love him, and
without seeing you now believe in him, and rejoice with inexpressible joy
touched with glory because you are achieving faith's goal, your salvation" (1 P 1:8-9). Others reject him: he is the sign of contradiction (Lk
2:34).

3.4.1 The historical Jesus. That Jesus actually lived is doubted today by
only a few people. No other person has been the object of such careful
and intensive research. Several authors and historians in the Roman
Empire mentioned him, both pagans (Suetonius, Tacitus, Pliny the
Younger, Lucian of Samosata, Celsus, Porphyry) and Jews (Flavius
Josephus and the authors of the *Talmud*). Josephus gives the most
detailed account in his book *Jewish Antiquities*, writing about 60 years
after the crucifixion. The version of this passage in the Greek text has
long been known to have been tampered with by Christian editors. The
authentic version was discovered in an Arabic text in the early 1970's
(Feb. 13, 1972 *New York Times*):

> At this time there was a wise man who was called Jesus. And his
> conduct was good, and [he] was known to be virtuous. And many
> people from among the Jews and other nations became his disci-
> ples. Pilate condemned him to be crucified and to die. And those
> who had become his disciples did not abandon his discipleship.
> They reported that he had appeared to them three days after his
> crucifixion and that he was alive: accordingly, he was perhaps the
> messiah concerning whom the prophets have recounted wonders.

But the most splendid testimony to Jesus is to be found in the books
of the New Testament. The Gospels were not intended to give a precise
factual narrative of the life of Jesus. They are not history books in the
modern sense. They are not simply biographies, either. Rather, they are
the early Church's books of testimony designed to awaken faith. The

Gospels recount the earthly life of Jesus from the point of view of the risen and exalted Christ. That is why it is necessary to distinguish between what Jesus lived and said and did, and the way in which all this was understood by the early Christian community which composed the Gospels.

3.4.2 Brief biography. The external events in the life of this man are quickly recounted. He was born in Bethlehem at the beginning of our new era. His home town was Nazareth. Here he spent his childhood and youth. Really, little is known about his earlier years. The childhood stories are not to be taken as strictly historical or historically exact narratives, in the present-day sense of the word (Mt 1:18-2:23; Lk 2:1-40). His parents were called Mary and Joseph. Joseph, at all events, was only his legal father. Jesus followed his foster-father's occupation. He was referred to as the "carpenter," and the "carpenter's son." Jesus' mother tongue was Aramaic. When Jesus was 30 years old, he appeared in public as a preacher. He assembled disciples, healed the sick, and worked other miracles. He caused considerable stir by associating with public sinners and the so-called rabble of his day. Through his behavior and his statements he came into conflict with the officials and the pious believers among the people. At about the age of 33 he was condemned to death after a mock trial. Shortly afterwards rumors were already circulating that he was alive again and had appeared to several of his followers.

3.4.3 "What kind of man is this?" (Mk 4:41). Jesus, as his contemporaries represented him, was not a zealot, not a gloomy moralizer, not a man out of touch with reality. He enjoys the flowers in the meadow and the birds in the sky. He observes the farmer when he sows and when he reaps. He is familiar with the everyday activities and customs of his countrymen. His love is tender, practical, and never theoretical (Mk 6:34, 8:2). He has sympathy for the poor, the sick and the outcast (Mk 2:40-42; Lk 7:22). He knows how to be happy (Lk 10:21), how to cry, and how to tremble with anxiety and agony (Jn 11:35; Mt 26:36-39).

This Jesus of Nazareth must have been a fascinating and most unusual man. He could tell a young man, "Come, follow me," and the young man would leave everything else behind. Strangers, too, and foreigners he drew into his spell. "We want to see Jesus," say the Greek foreigners (Jn 12:20-21). His friends were seized with amazement over and over again. They asked each other, "What kind of man is this?" (Mk 4:41). Even his enemies were deeply impressed with him: "It is evident

you do not act out of human respect but teach God's way of life sincerely"
(Mk 12:13-14). And everyone was amazed to discover that he was
teaching "like someone who had authority" (Mk 1:22). His words got
under their skin.

Jesus of Nazareth does not fit into any outline. He is wholly other. He
accepts the despised, the humble people, the public sinners, in friendship. He calls the little children to come to him, when his disciples are
trying to send them on their way. He stands by the adulterous woman,
when everyone else is condemning her (Jn 8:2-11). He turns away from
honor and glory when they try to make him king. He accepts a dinner
invitation from the hated tax collector—an unmistakable sign of friendship. He allows a prostitute to anoint his feet while he is at dinner in the
home of a respected family. He speaks with a Samaritan woman, even
though this was certain to be taken as heresy. He does not shrink from
touching the lepers, even though they were outcasts from human society. He holds his peace when they accuse him, when they mock him,
when they scourge him. His preaching and his teaching turn everything
upside down, and shock his audience: "When a person strikes you on the
right cheek, turn and offer him the other" (Mt 5:39). "If anyone wants to go
to law over your shirt, hand him your coat as well" (Mt 5:40). "Love your
enemies. Do good to those who hate you" (Mt 5:44). He is a contradiction
to the established order of society of his day. He has a weakness for the
weak (Mk 2:17; Lk 15). He himself lives from the vantage point of a wholly
unique relationship with God.

The unusual behavior and uncustomary life style of Jesus provoke
contradiction and resistance. His family regards him as a madman (Mk
3:21, 31). He is so far out of the normal that he is a source of embarrass-
ment to his relatives. His opponents characterize him as a carouser and
a drunkard (Lk 7:34). They determine to get rid of him, even though his
final and all-abiding concern is simply to achieve a new relationship
between God and man, and a new order among men.

3.4.4 Signs and wonders (Ac 4:30). In the New Testament, 35 separate
miracles are recounted. Some of them are described more than once
(there are a total of 62 miracle narratives). In addition, the New Testament records 18 composite miracle accounts. Jesus' miracles can be
divided into four groups: miracles involving nature, healings, raising of
the dead, and the driving out of devils. Jesus always tried to avoid what
we might call "show-miracles." His miracles were not designed to pro-
mote his reputation, but rather to bring God closer to man.

In reading the miracle stories, we are frequently tempted to ask only one question: did this all really happen the way it is written here? And thus, we often overlook the much more important question of what these miracles are supposed to mean. What is the good news they announce to us? These signs are to be evaluated in their true relationship with Jesus' salvific will and activity. By his words and his miracles, Jesus meant to invite mankind to believe. He wanted to confront them with a decision. "The Lord continued to work with them throughout and confirm the message through the signs which accompanied them" (Mk 16:20). These powerful deeds are signs for the dawning of a new era, the beginning of the kingdom of God: "The reign of God is already in your midst" (Lk 17:21).

3.5 Death and Resurrection

3.5.0 One day, Jesus was questioning his disciples: "Who do people say that I am?" "You are a prophet, a great man, a wise man." That is the opinion of the people. But Jesus will not be satisfied with this answer. "But you, who do you think I am?" This razor-sharp question demands a full declaration. And Peter formally confesses his faith: "You are the Christ, the Son of the living God" (Mt 16:16).

Christ belongs completely to God. He has come from God, as God's Son, and he lives with God. But he also fully represents the human side. For mankind, he has undertaken the boldest objective that anyone could set himself. For them, he died on the cross and rose again from the dead. Jesus is the "Man for God" and also, precisely for that reason, the "Man for men." "For us and for the sake of our salvation" . . . that is the summation of his whole life's purpose.

3.5.1 The ignominy of the cross. The focus and climax of the Old Testament Gospel was Israel's liberation from the bondage of Egypt. The focus and climax of the New Testament is the Gospel of redemption through Jesus Christ. This adventure of God with man seems to us like a remarkably splendid love story. Isaiah paints a gripping picture of the suffering servant of God: he has taken upon himself the burden of our sorrows. Bruised by suffering, he passes under the winepress and is crushed like a grape. (Is 52:13-53:12, 63:1-6). Love necessarily involves pain. At the end of his endurance, Jesus ranges back and forth in the Garden of Gethsemane. He complains that his soul is sorrowful unto death (Mk 14:34). He trembles in his agony, so that his sweat runs onto the ground like drops of blood. He begs for help: "Could you not watch a single hour with me?" (Mt 26:40).

This agony of God-made-Man is something impossible to grasp. Jesus is taken prisoner and condemned to the most horrible and shameful punishment known to his day, death on the cross. Like all capital offenders, he too is scourged before his crucifixion. Although terribly weakened from loss of blood, he is forced to carry his own cross out to the place of execution. When he arrives there, nails are driven through his hands and feet. The blood spurts out of his body. The cross is erected. Blood courses along the wet tree of the cross down onto the ground. Jesus experiences a sense of desertion so great that he cries out in the words of Psalm 22, "My God, why have you abandoned me?" (Mt 27:46). He is forced to fathom the meaninglessness of human life. He is made to have a terrible sense of the silence of God. Early in the afternoon of Good Friday he dies—the man on the cross. A soldier pierces his side in order to be certain that he is dead—the man on the cross. He does not die in his bed—the man on the cross.

3.5.2 "The folly of the cross" (1 Cor 1:18). Without comprehension, I stand before the incomprehensible mystery of the cross! "My child, what do you know about God?" the priest asked a little girl in catechism class. "I don't know, Father; I have always seen God suffering" (Leon Bloy). The oldest known representation of the crucified Jesus is a caricature that mocks the early Christians for worshipping a donkey. The crucified Jesus is, always, "for the heathens a folly" (1 Cor 1:23). The death of Jesus is, from a human point of view, an open scandal and nothing more. In his day, Jesus' closest friends were disturbed and shattered. For us Christians of today, the Crucifix is the most common representation of Jesus. Crucifixes hang in houses and churches; they stand at crossroads, in cemeteries, everywhere.

Without comprehension, I stand before the incomprehensible mystery of the cross! Is meaninglessness the meaning of the cross? Or is the cross a sign of bloody reparation? Is our God placated by blood? Is our God a heartless God, who finds his pleasure in suffering and death? The death of Jesus and the ignominy of the cross pose this question in an inexorable urgency. When all is said and done, there can be but one "explanation" of the cross: love. Christ was willing to pay something for friendship. He did not give only a handful of love. He gave all that he had. On Calvary everything speaks of love. The Redeemer's arms are spread wide, as if he meant to embrace the whole world in a gesture of love. His heart, the seat of love, is open, open to mankind. Red is the color of love. The cross is red, red from the redeeming blood of Christ. The cross is the great symbol of love, the symbol of redemption. "God so loved the world that he gave his only Son" (Jn 3:16). Thus the cross is the most powerful hymn of love; love that is not mere dalliance and play; love that paid the full price, life itself. Jesus' death on the cross is the greatest conceivable act of love. "He had loved his own in this world, and would show his love for them to the end" (Jn 13:1).

3.5.3 *Joy through the cross*. "I've always seen him suffering." That surely cannot be the whole picture. Jesus' dying prayer is: "Father, into your hands I commend my spirit" (Lk 23:46). His death is not an unrelieved leap into nothingness. He commits himself into the fatherly hands of God. That is why God's silence on Good Friday is not a silence any more. It is eloquently broken. "God freed him from death's bitter pangs, and raised him up again" (Ac 2:24). Jesus' death was a return to his Father, and a resurrection. God's love cannot be undone—not even on the cross. Easter changes everything. The crucifixion on Calvary is not simply a scandal story from the past. This loving surrender of the Redeemer is carried over into the present, and is destined to point to the future, even to the very eternity of God. The cross becomes the sign of Christ's victory and our consolation. "Through the wood of the Cross joy has come into the world" (Good Friday Liturgy). "With him is plenteous redemption" (Ps 130:7).

3.5.4 *Alleluia! Jesus lives!* Jesus Christ is risen and he is alive! Surely there is no other truth in the whole New Testament that is stressed so forcefully and so unequivocally. The Biblical witnesses to the Resurrection are numerous: the ancient formulas of faith (1 Cor 15; Rm 1:3-4, 10:9; Lk 24:34), the baptismal confessions and creeds (Ph 2:6-11; Ep 5:14; 1 Tm 3:16), the missionary preaching (Ac 2:14-40, 5:29-32, 10:34-43), and the Easter proclamations (Mt 28; Mk 16; Lk 24; Jn 20-21; Ac 1:3-11). On one point all these witnesses are agreed. They are not primarily interested in describing the event of resurrection. Rather, they want to proclaim Christ. These narratives are a confession of the Risen Savior who lives and who gives life.

3.5.5 *"And he has appeared to them" (cf. 1 Cor 15:5-7)*. Again and again the Risen Savior shows himself to his disciples. He speaks with them. They see him. They are allowed to touch him. It is not simply some spirit that is appearing to them (Lk 24:39). Christ is there, in person.

They recognize him. "It is the Lord" (Jn 21:7). Full of joy, they bring each other this happy news: "I have seen the Lord" (Jn 20:18, 25). They go out and "announce the good news to his followers, who were now grieving and weeping" (Mk 16:10).

The living Lord is none other than the Crucified Savior. That is why Christ shows himself to his friends with the marks of his wounds (Lk 24:40; Jn 20:20, 25, 27). In the light of the Resurrection, the disciples understand the cross of Good Friday. Only now on Easter, when they see the Lord, can they overcome the shock of the Crucifixion: "Why do you search for the living One among the dead?" (Lk 24:5).

Christ meets with them. They are beside themselves with joy and amazement (Lk 24:41). This meeting touches them in their innermost being, so that their life is completely altered. This, for example, was the case with St. Paul (Ac 9:1-22). These apparitions of the Risen Savior constitute the true foundation of the faith of the early Church: "And if Christ has not been raised, our preaching is void of content and your faith is empty too" (1 Cor 15:14).

There is something else that strikes us about the apparitions of the Lord. These men had, of course, once known Jesus personally. They had often seen him face to face. And now, a few days later, they apparently no longer know him. Even his most intimate friends ask each other if it is really the Lord. Something has changed. They can no longer experience this risen Christ as they would an earthly person. They can recognize Christ only in faith. St. Paul says it in direct and simple words: "We no longer look on anyone in terms of mere human judgment. If at one time we so regarded Christ, we no longer know him by this standard. . . . The old order has passed away; now all is new" (2 Cor 5:16-17).

3.5.6 "My Lord and my God" (Jn 20:28). These experiences of the Risen Savior give the disciples new heart. Once, they had left everything behind in order to follow this Jesus of Nazareth: family, work, friends. But on Good Friday they had lost everything. They all ran off when Jesus ended his life so wretchedly on the cross. They had imagined everything so differently! Their disillusionment knows no bounds. "We had hoped; and now . . ." (Lk 24:21). And now on Easter, suddenly everything is so totally different! Christ is alive! They can see him. The shock of Good Friday is overcome. They are seized with an indescribable joy.

Thomas, in a symbolic gesture, puts his hand into the open wound of the Redeemer. This "touching of the Risen Lord" causes him to confess his faith: "My Lord and my God" (Jn 20:28). The Credo of Jesus' friends does not revolve primarily around the Resurrection itself. That is why they do not make the slightest attempt to recount the process of the Resurrection as observers and witnesses. For them, this is a matter of only secondary importance. Their concern is for the Risen Lord himself, for their understanding of who he is (2 Cor 5:16), and for their friendship with him. He himself inspires them. They call him "our Lord" (Ph 2:11; 1 P 1:3).

3.5.7 Living and rising with the Lord. In Jesus the incomprehensible love of God has bodily taken root among us. And thus, it is part and parcel of his destiny that he should be fought over. Neither the early Church nor the Church of today, neither the faithful nor the non-believers are "finished with him." After Easter the disciples see the Lord. They believe in the Risen Savior. They do not need lengthy explanations. For them, Christ is not an object of discussion; he is the Christ of their faith.

My faith, today, must indeed be mature and critical. But still, it must not be only a mere basis of questions and investigation, riddles and the search for proof. Believing in Christ consists, rather, in my trusting surrender to him, and in my seeking for his redeeming closeness. For now, I must still follow him along the Way of the Cross. I must take up my cross day after day, and suffer and die with Christ (Lk 9:23, 14:27; 2 Cor 4:10; Ph 3:10). But I cherish the hope that I shall rise again with Christ (1 Cor 15; Ph 3:20-21), destined someday to enjoy his friendship forever.

4. KNOWING GOD: KNOWING WHAT HE SAYS (GOD'S WORD)

4.0 "We have found out today that a man can still live after God has spoken with him" (Dt 5:24).

4.1 Word as encounter

The man who loves, seeks for contact with the beloved in a multitude of ways, and tries to converse with them. It is primarily through words that I open my heart to another person and communicate with them. My word is my self-surrender to another person. Words can carry love and hatred, joy and sorrow from one heart to another. Words can make happy and heal; they can wound and kill. "Life and death are in the power of the tongue" (Pr 18:21; cf. Jm 3).

It is a fact of human experience that people in love "understand" each other best. When I have confidence in someone, I interpret their words with my heart. If I understand the words of my beloved well, these words can increase the love within me. And thus the decisive element is not so much what someone says, as who it is that speaks. When two people say something alike, they do not necessarily say exactly the same thing. In a conversation that turns into a genuine meeting of minds, three levels have to coincide: what is said (I believe what you say), trust (I believe you), and the person of the speaker (I believe in you).

4.2 The Word of God

Something similar can be said of God's Word. When God reveals himself and begins to speak, he expresses himself, and he wants to meet me. That is why Christian faith is also a "faith in expression." The so-called "faith as knowledge" is certainly not something secondary. It is not enough that I believe; I must also believe something. In all this, it is naturally the speaking Person of God who enjoys the absolute pre-eminence. Hearing the word of God turns into meeting with God whenever I understand with the heart and, progressing beyond the words, recognize the loving Person of God. "Indeed, God's word is living and effective, sharper than any two-edged sword. It penetrates and divides soul and spirit, joints and marrow; it judges the reflections and thoughts of the heart" (Heb 4:12).

4.3 The Incarnate Word of God

"In times past, God spoke in fragmentary and varied ways to our fathers through the prophets; in this, the final age, he has spoken to us through his Son" (Heb 1:1-2). Indeed, God expresses himself in his Son. In him, God has spoken more than words. Jesus Christ is the Word of God absolutely, the highest possible revelation of God. "And the Word became Flesh" (Jn 1:14). That is why Christ can say of himself: "I am the truth" (Jn 14:6). He speaks about God, not in barren theories, but in a way that causes everyone to be amazed, because he was teaching "like someone who had authority" (Mt 7:28-29). His friends have a presentiment of who it is that is speaking to them: "Lord, to whom should we go? You have the words of eternal life" (Jn 6:68).

4.4 God's Word in writing

4.4.0 God and believing men have also given us a book which we call the "Word of God," or the Bible.

4.4.1 The Bible. The English word "Bible" comes from the Greek word "biblos" which means simply "the book." The Bible itself is always regarded as God's word in human words. The book is an old one. According to recent figures, it has been translated into 1685 languages. It is properly the book of the Christian Church. This writing dates from very different eras. The Song of Deborah (Jg 5) is probably the oldest text. It dates from the eleventh century B.C. The Second Epistle of Peter is the most recent book of the Bible (written about 120 A.D.). Between the oldest and the most recent texts, there is a time span of more than 1200 years. The Old Testament has 46 books, and the New Testament has 27.

4.4.2 The Old Testament. The Old Testament was not composed at some author's desk. Among the Jews of those days, the father of a family would tell his children about the great deeds that God had performed for their ancestors. In this way, these traditions were handed down from one generation to the other. Over and over again, these witnesses to faith were collected and written down by scribes during that stage of the Bible's development. The Biblical writer is not simply recording history; he is trying to encourage his contemporaries to maintain their faith in the true God. The entire Old Testament is one grand dialogue between God and man, between the past and future generations.

4.4.3 The New Testament. The Gospels, too, are not primarily historical accounts about Jesus. They are not reportage, but the good news of salvation. They were not composed until some decades after Christ's Resurrection. This does not mean that the Gospels are historically unreliable. The Evangelists record for us the person of Jesus, who actually did live a human life as they describe. These books do not always record Jesus' words verbatim, but still they contain his authentic message.

In the Gospels, we encounter Jesus the Christ. The historical Jesus, however, is interpreted there as the Christ of our faith in the light of the Resurrection. In them, we learn to know the Savior who lives as the Risen Lord.

The remaining books of the New Testament record the life of the Christian communities after the Resurrection of Christ. They give us an insight into the era in which the Church came into being. Here we see the record of a new experience of God by man: the experience of the Risen Lord who is alive and present. They give us a presentiment of the new life with Christ.

4.5 "Words taught by the Spirit" (1 Cor 2:13)

4.5.0 From the first to the last page of the Bible, we encounter the Spirit of God. Already the second verse of Scripture speaks of the "Spirit of God" (Gn 1:2).

4.5.1 *"The Spirit of Truth" (Jn 16:13).* Holy Scripture is God's word in human words, because the Holy Spirit was at work in the Biblical writers, so that the texts were written under his primary influence (Jn 20:31; 2 Tm 3:16; 1 P 1:10-12; 2 P 1:20-21, 3:15-16). We call this process inspiration. "The Spirit scrutinizes all matters, even the deep things of God. . . . No one knows what lies at the depths of God but the Spirit of God" (1 Cor 2:10-11). It is he who incites and directs the authors, so that they can faithfully and accurately teach the truths that God himself wants to be recorded in Sacred Scripture for our salvation. Thus, in the last analysis, both of them are the authors of Scripture, God and the human writer.

4.5.2 *"Do not stifle the Spirit" (1 Th 5:19).* After the Resurrection of Christ, the Spirit is at work primarily in the community of the faithful (Jn 14:16-17, 15:26, 16:13-15). He turns the scattered disciples of Jesus into the Church of Christ. He makes possible the faith in the Risen Savior. Every manifestation of life in the Church comes from the activity of the Spirit: Baptism, the preaching of the Gospel, the forgiveness of sins, and the charismatic graces. "There are different gifts, but the same Spirit" (1 Cor 12:4). The Spirit of Truth is to introduce the Church of Christ into the truth. "He will not speak on his own, but will speak only what he hears, and will announce to you the things to come. In doing this he will give glory to me, because he will have received from me what he will announce to you" (Jn 16:13-14).

The Holy Spirit thus has a twofold mission in the people of God. First, he is to remind the Church of the words and activity of Christ, and thus make them present (Jn 14:26, 15:26, 16:13). The decisive thing is that Jesus be recognized, today, as Redeemer and Lord (1 Cor 12:3). Next, the Spirit is to announce what is destined to come (Jn 16:13). His reminding us of Christ continues into the most distant future, "until the Lord comes again" in power and glory.

4.6 God's Word in human words

4.6.0 In the Bible I can read man's word and God's word at one and the same time. I can understand what men have written, and I can understand what God wants to say to me.

4.6.1 Literary genres. God's message to man is a single and consistent narrative of love. But the book in which this message is couched consists of a collection of the most diverse pieces of writing, all of which can be distinguished by their various literary genres. It contains historical books, compilations of laws, prophetic books, didactic writings, parables, chronicles, Gospels, collected letters, and apocalyptic writings.

4.6.2 Sitz im Leben. Even the so-called "Sitz im Leben" (a technical term for the situation in life of the authors of the books of the Bible), is important for a proper understanding of the individual books of Scripture. The Bible is a very old book. Much of what is said there seems alien to us. There is much that no longer fits into our world view and conception of life. Many of our contemporaries have the impression that such a "word of God" is an insult to our intelligence.

The Biblical writers obviously had no inkling in their day of our modern natural sciences. At the same time, many typically oriental ways of thinking have worked their way into the Bible. We have a hard time today trying to grasp the thought processes and manners of expression familiar to these writers of an earlier age. It is also important to know whether the individual books and parts of books were originally spoken as sermons or intended for instruction and divine service.

4.6.3 Purpose of the author. If, accordingly, we are to correctly understand the individual books of Scripture, we must pay careful attention to the real purpose and objective of the author. Considerable confusion has already been occasioned in the Church, simply because people have looked at Scripture as a history book in the present-day sense of the word. The Bible is meant to be neither a book of natural science nor a book in which historically verifiable facts are recounted. It is rather a book of faith. The Biblical writers did not write as reporters, but as believers. And their writings are confessions: wondering, grateful confessions of faith vis-a-vis the wonderful deeds of God.

4.6.4 Two examples.

A.) In the first book of the Bible. The creation narrative in Genesis must not be understood literally. For example, as if God had created the world in 7 times 24 hours. The author does not mean to present a narrative of how the world was created. What he wants to say is, nonetheless, quite true. He is concerned simply with one definite statement of faith: creation is a work of God. God says yes to the world, and thus the world is good.

This same Biblical narrative is not intended to record how man came into being, but to tell us what man is. "The Lord God formed man out of the clay of the ground and blew into his nostrils the breath of life" (Gn 2:7). That is, man too is a creature of God: he owes his life to the Creator God. On the one hand, he is related to the world of matter (earth). The Hebrew word "Adam" means equivalently "man from the earth." Man is transitory, and can turn back into earth again through death. But on the other hand, man is also the partner of God. He has received his breath of life personally and immediately from God. There is therefore an essential distinction between man and animal (Gn 2:18-20).

And when God takes woman from man's rib (Gn 2:21-25), all that means is that man and woman are both of equal worth, if not of equal form and figure. In the ancient Near East, women were not worth very much. The Biblical author is warning us against this under-evaluation of woman. Thus, he makes it unequivocally clear that both man and woman are full and complete human beings.

B.) From the last book of the Bible. In writing the book of Revelation, John did not have the intention of composing a fantastic novel of the future. He was writing a letter of consolation to his oppressed brethren in the faith, to give them courage. The Kingdom of God will triumph, for the final and decisive victory of God has already begun with the Resurrection of Christ. The goal of history can therefore only be the completion and revelation of this victory.

4.6.5 "God's word is living and effective" (Heb 4:12). "Oracle of the Lord," "God said": No fewer than 241 times do we find expressions like this in Scripture. I meet the word of God clad in the impoverished garb of human words, and that is why it has its weaknesses.

And still it is a Creator-Word, filled with divine power (Ep 6:17; Rv 1:16, 2:12, 19:15). Already in the Old Testament this creative power of God's word is often called to mind. "So shall my word be that goes forth from my mouth; it shall not return to me void, but shall do my will, achieving the end for which I sent it" (Is 55:11). "He spoke, and it was made" (Ps 33:9). "At God's word were his works brought into being" (Si 42:15; cf. Si 42:15-43:35; Ws 9:1; Ps 33:6).

On the other hand, this same word of God has the power to kill and to annihilate. "Is not my word like fire, says the Lord, like a hammer shattering rocks?" (Jr 23:29; cf. Is 11:4; Ho 6:5; Ws 18:15-16; 2 Th 2:8).

The word is like a "judge over the reflections and thoughts of the heart" (Heb 4:12). "Whoever rejects me and does not accept my words already has his judge, namely, the word I have spoken—it is that which will condemn him on the last day" (Jn 12:48).

The word of God is also a saving word. "Whoever hears and keeps my word will not see death for ever" (Jn 5:24, 8:51; cf. Ps 107:20). The words of God are "words of life and salvation" (Ph 2:16; Jn 6:68; Ac 13:26), for "not on bread alone is man to live but on every utterance that comes from the mouth of God" (Mt 4:4; Dt 8:3). The Word and the salvation-giving Spirit are bound up with each other (Lk 1:31; Jn 1:14). And "it is the power of God leading everyone who believes in it to salvation" (Rm 1:16). "Your words . . . became the joy and happiness of my heart" (Jr 15:16).

4.6.6 "Faith comes from hearing" (Rm 10:17). The Risen Savior gave his disciples this mandate: "Go into the whole world and proclaim the good news to all creation. The man who believes in it and accepts baptism will be saved" (Mk 16:15-16). "Faith, then, comes from hearing, and what is heard is the word of Christ" (Rm 10:17).

Thus the word of God plays a significant role in the life of the individual believer and in the community of the faithful. The Church, for her part, is also the incarnation of the word of God. For Christ wants to be present, not only in the books of the Bible, but in the hearts of the faithful. It is, to a considerable degree, dependent upon the Church whether the word of God is "hearable" for mankind today. One of the most important mandates of the Church's teaching office consists in explaining the word of God for mankind today, and keeping guard over the correct method of interpreting the Scriptures.

Hearing is the first answer to the word. How often we find that simple invitation in the Bible: "Hear" (Mt 7:24, 13:18; Lk 8:8). Mary, the sister of the busy Martha, sits at our Lord's feet and listens to his word (Lk 10:38-42). The man who listens meets with the man who speaks. "If anyone hears me calling and opens the door, I will enter his house" (Rv 3:20).

The word effects an encounter. That is why we must "listen with the heart." Solomon the Wise wanted to have "a hearing heart." And this wish was pleasing to God (1 K 3:5-14). The decisive element is the heart. For the man of today with his over-reliance on the head, it might very well be a good idea to try to listen with his heart as well as his head.

The pious Israelites used to invite each other to prayer with these words: "Hear his voice. Do not harden your hearts" (Ps 95:7-8). Moses enjoyed familiarity with God and could speak to him "face to face, as one man speaks to another" (Ex 33:11; Dt 34:10). This kind of hearing leads to obedience, as we find it so beautifully expressed in Peter's simple formula of faith and trust: "If you say so" (Lk 5:5).

5. RECOGNIZING GOD (ENCOUNTER WITH GOD)

5.0 The English word "religion" probably comes from the Latin word *religare*, which means "to bind." Knowing the truths of faith, and holding them for truth, might well be a proper and very important objective. These "truths," however, can achieve their purpose only when they lead to an encounter with the living God. Christian faith is an event that lays its claim upon my entire person, and binds me to the Person of God. Only on the basis of this encounter can the knowledge of faith achieve its proper warmth and soul.

5.1 "Know the Lord" (Heb 8:11; Jr 31:34)

5.1.0 Christian faith thus consists not so much in a rational understanding, as in a recognition of the Lord (Ep 4:13; Col 2:2). The Biblical concept of recognition has a very definite meaning: it means meeting the partner in the most intimate surrender of love; completely grasping a loving "You" with our heart; entering into a living relationship and a most intimate exchange with the other; experiencing this other person in a loving manner. The Bible says, for example, of Adam: "The man knew his wife Eve and she conceived and bore Cain" (Gn 4:1). And of Cain: "Cain knew his wife and she conceived and bore Enoch" (Gn 4:17). And the question asked by the Virgin Mary, "How can this be since I do not know man?" (Lk 1:34), is to be interpreted in this same light.

In much the same manner, Scripture depicts faith as an act of "knowing God." That is, an understanding that proceeds from the innermost self; as an encounter of love and unity with God; as a lived relationship and friendly exchange with Christ; as a trusting surrender of self to the Risen Lord. The Bible portrays faith in words and images of love: "Seek the face of the Lord" (Ps 105:4). "We must make known the glory of God shining on the face of Christ" (2 Cor 4:6). "We must achieve friendship with Christ" (2 Cor 5:20). Faith is thus, essentially, a blessed exclamation of wonder and love: "How deep are the riches and the wisdom and the knowledge of God!" (Rm 11:33).

5.1.1 Believing with the heart. The word "heart" is used quite often in the Bible. This expression refers to the innermost part of a man, the place where man is, in the last analysis, truly man. Often the same thought is expressed by the words "bowels" or "kidneys," etc. "God, who scrutinizes the heart and kidneys" (Ps 7:10). And thus the heart is also the place of encounter with God. "We believe with the heart" (Rm 10:9-10). And with Christ: "May Christ dwell in your hearts through faith and may charity be the root and foundation of your life. Thus you will be able to grasp fully, with all the holy ones, the breadth and length and height and depth of Christ's love, and experience this love which surpasses all knowledge" (Ep 3:17-19).

5.1.2 Into the inner self. If Christ is present in the depths of my heart, then I must try to meet with him and bind myself gently to him. There, Christ does not offer me stones instead of bread. He offers me friendship and community. Has not the man of today lost something of his soul and inner sensitivity? Conversion is a journey into the inner self. It is an act of growing in "grace and the knowledge of the Lord" (2 P 3:18). It is a returning home, into the innermost depths of self, to find self and Christ once again.

This conversion of faith has many names: trust, preparedness, surrender, faithfulness, obedience (2 Tm 4.7; 1 P 1:6-9; Rm 1:5, 4:18-25; Heb 11). It naturally extends much further than mere moral correctness and the fulfillment of the obligations imposed by the Church. Trust is the most beautiful gift that I can ever give a friend. The conversion of faith is the trusting decision of a person who has been moved by God.

5.1.3 Meditation: finding oneself. One way to accomplish this trip into the inner self is by meditation. Our life today is measured by clocks and productivity. We live in the midst of noise and constant activity. Many a man has lost his innermost identity and his sense of belonging. He lives only on the surface. This can lead to a feeling of emptiness, and a sort of homesickness for one's real self. Many people would like to revisit themselves, to be a guest in their own selves.

It is through silence and the cessation of activity, through contemplating a picture or listening to serious music, through meditation, in a word, that I go deep into myself. This path into myself is like a blessed

journey into my soul. Over and over again, I can find and experience my own self. This knowledge of my innermost self is necessary for my complete meeting with another person. In this experience, the entire person is at work. Meditation is totality. One of the most important things about it is breathing. Breath is more than air. It is life itself. "God blew the breath of life into his nostrils and so man became a living being" (Gn 2:7). Through relaxation and concentration, through a perfectly erect and at the same time relaxed sitting posture (for example, the lotus position), I can experience myself. I am simply there—and I can learn to accept myself as I am. Only when I have thus found myself, can I submit myself properly recollected to a face-to-face encounter. Thus meditation is geared towards communication, and can also be a genuine encounter with God.

5.1.4 Meeting with God. Meeting with each other means mutually giving and accepting the gift of self. When all is said and done, it is on the basis of encounters such as this that a man lives. Christian faith, too, is above all else an encounter. It is only secondarily a theology. To put it in other words, faith is not the successful result of my deliberations or the conclusion of a rational series of demonstrations. Encounter permits the invisible and the incomprehensible to enter into my life. And in this process, my own going towards God is not the first thing. The Old Testament already speaks of God as the one who takes the initiative, who "comes" and "appears" in order to speak (Ex 19:9), to bless (Ex 20:24), to judge (Ps 96:13), and to redeem (Is 59:19-21).

Through the Incarnation of his Son, God has taken a final and definitive step towards man. Since that moment Christ is firmly rooted in humanity, and humanity in Christ. The greatest conceivable presence of the Lord and the unheard-of union with him are possible only through the Resurrection. The Gospel of St. Matthew does not conclude with a formula of departure. Quite the contrary. Before his Ascension, Christ gave this assurance to his followers: "I am with you all days" (Mt 28:20). This ever-abiding closeness of the Lord is of the essence of God's faithfulness to man. Christ invites us: "Come to me" (Mt 11:28), and "abide in me" (Jn 15:4).

To be a trusted companion and to serve as such—this is a fundamental human experience. The two disciples on the road to Emmaus enjoy the companionship of the Risen Savior along their way. When they arrive at their village, they beg Christ, their unknown fellow traveler: "Stay with us" (Lk 24:29).

He meets with his own especially in community. "Where two or three are gathered together in my name, there am I in their midst" (Mt 18:20). The Church (*Ecclesia*, that is, those called together) is the assembly of brothers and sisters around the Lord who lives in their midst.

The Risen Savior is still alive. He is waiting for me. He calls me by my name. He comes to me in a thousand ways: in the joys of this life, in the smile of a child, in the crying of a poor man, in the picture of a starving man. The decisive element is always the same: I must become engaged with this person, not just to talk about him, but to live with him.

5.1.5 Intimacy of heart. True meeting between two people in love means "knowing" and uniting in an intimacy of the heart. Christian faith is a lived relationship with Christ, a mutual act of knowing each other. "I know mine and mine know me. They know my voice and listen to it" "If anyone loves me, I will love him in return and reveal myself to him" (Jn 14:21). Faith is a loving act of "touching the Lord" (cf. Jn 20:17), a surrender to him, such that "nothing can separate me from the love of God, which is in Jesus Christ our Lord" (Rm 8:38-39). And thus in faith both intimacy of heart and tenderness have a role to play. The qualities must not, however, be confused with sentimentality and emotionalism.

It is no accident that the whole content of the Bible can be summed up in the word "covenant." The covenant is a relationship of trust between persons. The covenant of marriage finds its deepest expression in the loving surrender, in the physical union of the lovers. God's covenant, for its part, finds its fulfillment in God's becoming one with man, to the point where "the Word was made Flesh" (Jn 1:14). "Lord, where do you live? Come and see" (Jn 1:38-39). "We will make our dwelling place with him" (Jn 14:23). Living together means real trust, being close to each other, knowing and loving each other, being there for each other in a community of love and living.

"I am the vine, you are the branches. He who lives in me and I in him, will produce abundantly, for apart from me you can do nothing" (Jn 15:5). This comparison also describes faith as friendship: a union with the Lord, joined together with him in mutual love. "In him and with him and through him."

5.1.6 Gestures of love. Every genuine love requires gestures. Love needs to express itself in words and gestures of love. I cannot imagine a romance in which the lovers do not caress and embrace and kiss each other. When these signs of love do not come from the heart, they are caricatures and lies. They are empty husks, because they neither express love nor do they bring love into being. In much the same way, religious practices (such as prayer and the sacraments) are genuine signs of faith only when they are filled with the warmth of a believing heart, and lead to a meeting with the living Lord.

5.2 Sacraments: signs of faith

5.2.0 The word "sacrament" means "mystery" or "sacred thing." Originally it comes from the Latin word *sacer* (something holy and untouchable because it has been dedicated to God). In antiquity, whenever anyone went to court he had to deposit a definite sum of money in a sanctuary. If he lost the case, the money belonged to the deity. He regarded it as a holy, inalienable and untouchable object (sacrament), because God and man had bound themselves together in it. The Christians took over this word and gave it a very special meaning. In our books of faith, the concept of sacrament is described as follows: a visible sign, instituted by Christ, by which invisible grace is communicated to us.

Unfortunately, far too many Christians of today have almost wholly lost their feeling for these "signs of the faith." "A person might almost think that we had lost the key of the door which separates the sacrament world from us" (Bruno Hidber).

In the following paragraphs it is not my concern to present an abridged treatise on the sacraments. I shall simply attempt to point out one possible approach to the mystery of the sacraments. Then I will take examples from Baptism, the Eucharist and Penance to illustrate the fact that our sacraments are signs of faith and personal friendship with Christ.

5.2.1 *Getting to know others.* Nobody has so successfully outlined the approach to sacrament as Antoine de Saint-Exupery. In his book *The Little Prince*, he writes that people today no longer have the time to get to know things. They buy everything ready-made at the store. Then, since there are no marketplaces for friends, people do not have friends. The Little Prince went to the 5,000 roses:

> "You are not at all like my rose," he said. "As yet you are nothing. No one has tamed you, and you have tamed no one.... You are beautiful, but you are empty," he went on. "One could not die for you. To be sure, an ordinary passerby would think that my rose looked just like you—the rose that belongs to me. But in herself alone she is more important than all the hundreds of you other roses because it is she that I have watered.... Because she is *my* rose."

And the fox said, "And now here is my secret, a very simple secret: It is only with the heart that one can see rightly; what is essential is invisible to the eye."

5.2.2 Touching upon Mystery. One day, a young man admitted to me:

> "For a long time, I have been looking for a proof of God that would be self-evident to me. Now I have found it. I touch upon the mystery everywhere: in the smile of a child and the agony of a dying man; in the song of a bird and the blossoming of a tree; in the smallness of an atom and the vastness of the universe; in man's love and hate. Ultimately, I cannot understand any of this. I touch upon mystery everywhere. Must it not be true that all these mysteries merge into one great mystery, which I call God?"

A person who meets the world of things with wonder and an open heart learns that they are as transparent as glass, and that they all have a voice. In them, he can have a presentiment of mystery. They turn into a sort of "sacrament" for him.

For the believing Christian, these things take on an even deeper meaning. Through the Incarnation, God has boldly made himself a part of the world, in Christ. God has united himself with the visible creation. Since that moment, Jesus Christ is the original Sacrament, the meeting point and place of encounter between God and man. He is and remains the sign in which we recognize and experience God's care for us.

All sacraments are thus based in Jesus Christ. They are simply radiations of this prime Sacrament. In them, the Incarnation of God is somehow carried further. Water and oil, bread and wine, are a part of our visible world. In the sacraments, they become palpable signs of the reality beyond our grasp: signs and tools of faith, in which I touch upon mystery.

5.2.3 Signs that live. My parents' house is an ancient wooden building. My grandparents and great-grandparents on my mother's side already lived in it. I myself was born in it. There I spent my childhood years. The faded walls with the original streaks are dear and intimate to me. I have often looked at them fleetingly or in silent wonder. Their image has imprinted itself indelibly upon my heart.

Even today, I am unaccountably drawn to the memory of this house. Every time I go into the living room, I still—after 50 years—feel a warmth in my heart. It is as if I saw in these wooden walls the faces of my dead parents and grandparents. These old beams come to life; they have a heart and a voice; they tell me a story of my own childhood. I remember the days and the holidays that I spent in this room. I remember games I played there, and tears I shed there. Memory is a powerful language which tells me about the past from within my own self. It is as if I had lost a piece of myself within these four walls, and had just found it again. In these things, my own childhood, my own parents and grandparents are as close to me as if they were present at this very moment. In a word, my parents' house is a "sacrament" for me. It is similar to ten other houses in my home village. And still, it is precisely this one old wooden building that is so unique for me. These beams are more precious to me than all the wood that anyone could every buy. Signs can live.

A person who had no relationship to this tumble-down old home, a person who had never been on intimate terms with this wood—for such a person these walls would have no meaning, and nothing to tell. Then these same things become empty and dumb and dead. For him they are no signs, no symbols.

5.2.4 Signs of friendship. One day, two young people meet. It is the beginning of a great love. The external story of this love can be described, but the inner story remains ultimately an unfathomable mystery. The lovers have their own language. They hold hands, they caress and kiss each other. They write letters to each other, or they keep meeting each other. Often in the same place. This place becomes more and more intimate for them. They give each other presents. Often just trifles. But in these things, they give up their hearts to one another. Items like these, in and of themselves, can be found and bought anywhere. But for people in love, they are priceless, precious. "We can see well only with the heart. The essentials are invisible to the eye." The person in love can sense in these things the presence of his beloved. Memory is the language of hidden attentions.

The places of their earlier meetings, or the things they gave each other, remain unique and special, even later. These things call the entire story of their love to memory: they become the signs of their closeness. In these external signs we can read, as in a mirror, how the two of them stand in their interior relationship together. The things they gave each other remain alive. They are passage-ways through which their love can go from one heart to the other. And these visible signs, these "memories," are constantly at work to sustain and increase their love and affection. In a word, these signs of friendship are valued no longer simply in terms of their usefulness. They become "sacraments" for the two people in love.

5.2.5 Signs of faith. All this helps me to understand the seven sacraments of the Church. God is the Wholly Other, the Invisible and Incomprehensible. But, in his boundless love, he wants to be near us. God's history with man is a history of love which extends over the course of centuries. It reaches a climax in the Incarnation: God brings man into his intimacy. Bible and Church are two living reminders of this history and presence of God's love. In faith, I thus can sense this closeness of God from within.

As a man, I am dependent upon visible signs. Even in an industrialized world, I express unity and hope and festive joy in signs. If they are wanting, my human life is that much poorer. As a believer, too, I need some sensible sign to nourish and express my inner attitudes. God knows this. That is why he, the Invisible, turns to me in visible signs, in order to give himself to me in Christ. These signs are not only the medium through which I receive "something"; they bring me into living contact with God. As a believer, I accept this gift of encounter in freedom and gratitude. These signs of faith and of God's closeness are called sacraments. Things of this world, like water, bread and wine become signs and bearers of a different, divine reality. In them, there is a meeting between the powerful activity of God and the preparedness of man. These holy signs are signs of faith because on the one hand they presuppose faith, and on the other hand they nourish and develop it.

5.2.6 Signs can speak. An object that lovers give each other becomes for them a source of memory. The gift has a voice for them: it can speak and join them together.

In a similar way, the sacramental sign is transparent for the believer. It can speak. I encounter God not with the object itself (for example, the bread in the Eucharist), but in and through the object. In these signs of faith, the ongoing history of God with man is called to memory and made present. In them, I encounter the personal Being of God. In them, he gives himself to me and offers me redemption. In the sacrament, I am taken into a thousand-year-long history of love. Things meaningless in themselves take on, for the believer, an absolutely unique value.

The uninitiated will see, in the Eucharistic bread, simply a piece of bread. For a believing Christian, however, it is the "living bread" (Jn 6:51). This holy sign is alive; it reminds me of the boundless love of Christ for me; in it I meet with the Redeemer who wants to be close to me and who unites himself to me: it is the body of the Risen Lord. "I am the living bread. . . . He who eats my flesh and drinks my blood will have everlasting life and I will raise him up on the Last Day. . . . He who eats this bread will live forever" (Jn 6:51-58).

Signs, words and actions mutually clarify and enhance each other.

For people in love, the presents they have exchanged, their gestures of affection, and their words of love all mutually complete and explain each other. Their signs and words and actions are an expression and enhancement of their love.

Thus, in the Sacrament of the Eucharist, I am made to understand that the Savior is bodily present to me, to be my nourishment for eternal life. The sign (bread), the words ("This is my Body"), and the action (eating) all together speak the same language. Taken all together, they are able to express what any single one of them could not succeed in doing without the others.

5.2.7 Celebrating God's closeness in community. The sacraments are signs of God's love and closeness. In them, so to speak, the Incarnation of God continues to work. Through them, the Church fulfills its mandate to make redemption present to the believers of today in the "signs of faith." In the sacraments the faithful, all together, celebrate the gift of God and the answer of man. That is why the celebration of a sacrament should always be a blessed community experience.

5.2.8 Living—Believing—Celebrating. In every country, in every people and tribe, the great events of life—birth, marriage, death—are celebrated in community. Unfortunately, many Christians today no longer experience the fact that, in the sacraments of the Church, "life is celebrated in faith." There is a considerable gap between religion and life; between what we live and what we believe; between what we believe and what we celebrate.

The Council of Trent has solemnly declared that the sacraments in the strict sense of the word are: Baptism, Confirmation, Eucharist, Penance, Anointing of the Sick, Holy Orders and Matrimony. They are all of them unequivocally oriented towards life. Birth and maturity, nourishment and banquet, love and fidelity, guilt and forgiveness, sickness and death, mediation between man and God—these are the key points in human life. It is precisely here, in these pivotal moments of our existence, that the sacraments have their bearing. And thus, God is there with his redeeming love at the most important stages of our life. The seven sacraments show how radically serious God is about our human life.

The sacraments must not be separated from the day-by-day activity of Christian living. Rather, they all spring from this daily living and they all refer back to it. Through the celebration of the sacraments, life situations and life processes are made conscious, grasped in their deeper meanings, and sanctified. The sacramental celebrations, for their part, are supposed to lead us to the service of our fellow man and all the world. At the same time, the sacraments are oriented towards creation and all of life, because they are rooted in the manifold forms of man's meeting with the cosmos, in man's behavior with his fellow man, and in man's relationship with God. The sacraments are at the same time the climax and focus of all these relationships. Living—believing—celebrating.

5.3 Baptism: children of God

5.3.0 "Each of you is a son of God because of your faith in Christ Jesus. All of you who have been baptized into Christ have clothed yourselves with him. . . . All are one in Christ!" (Gal 3:26-28).

5.3.1 The holy waters. I grew up in a small mountain village. In summer, when the sun glowed mercilessly, the fields and meadows of these sunny mountains were often completely parched and withered. Plants and grass all died. For centuries, the mountain people had brought in water from many miles away to irrigate the fields and meadows. "Holy water"—that is what they called the water flowing in their irrigation works. Without water, there would be no harvest; there would be no life. And thus, for me, from my very earliest years, water was "holy," the symbol of life.

5.3.2 Water "unto eternal life." In the sign of life-giving water, God, in Baptism, gives us his life through the Holy Spirit. Thereby the baptized person becomes a child of God. He joins with the Living Savior in his death and in his Resurrection. He is received into the visible community of the People of God, in which all are brothers and sisters of the Lord. "It was in one Spirit that all of us, whether Jew or Greek, slave or free, were baptized into one body" (1 Cor 12:13).

5.4 Eucharist: meeting the Lord

5.4.0 The eternally faithful love of God has become visible for us in the life, death, and Resurrection of Jesus Christ. Since his Resurrection, Christ has indeed withdrawn from our sense experience. But his love forces him to continue to give himself to mankind. As the Risen Savior, he remains present for us in the Sacrament.

5.4.1 Eucharist: memorial to the Lord. The hour is solemn. On the day before his death, Jesus gathers his friends in the room of the Last Supper. For the last time, he eats and drinks with them. He lets them feel his closeness, and experience his love. Then he gives his disciples the ultimate gift: a memorial of himself. He invites them to assemble in remembrance of him: "Do this in memory of me" (1 Cor 11:24).

Friendship lives on memories. Genuine friendship is a continuous memory of the experiences enjoyed with the one we love. "Remember, be mindful!" Like a refrain, this invitation to remember rings through the entire Bible. What is involved is not simply thinking back to what has happened earlier. When the Jewish father would tell his family the story of the liberation from bondage in Egypt, he was thereby building a bridge from the past to the present: God had done this in the past for our fathers; we glorify his name because he is close to us today in his love. "Remember!"

Jesus, too, wants his followers to remember him. On Holy Thursday, he left behind a memorial for his disciples: "Do this in memory of me." On Easter, Christ appears to these same friends. He who died on the cross out of love is now alive. They can meet with him. Their hearts burn within them when they recognize him in the breaking of the bread (Lk 24:13-35). The first Christians live on the strength of this food.

Today, when the priest reads the account of the institution of the Eucharist during the liturgy, what he is recounting is not past history. This remembering of the hour of the Last Supper (in faith and in the sacramental sign) is an encounter with the Risen Lord. This memorial is the Risen Lord himself: "This is my Body" (Lk 22:19). Faith is friendship!

5.4.2 Eucharist: becoming one with the Lord. The meal is a sign of life, of community and unity. The memorial meal of the Eucharist is also called "communion." Communion means "uniting," "joining together," "community." It is here that the believer finds his most intense union with Christ. For Christians, the Eucharist is the core and climax of their encounter with God. In this mystery of the faith, in this self-surrender of Christ, the Lord himself makes real his invitation: "Abide in me." "The man who feeds on my flesh and drinks my blood remains in me, and I in him" (Jn 6:56). "The man who feeds on this bread shall live forever" (Jn 6:58). In the sign of the sacrament I can recognize him "with the eyes of the heart" (Ep 1:18). Faith is friendship!

5.4.3 Eucharist: One Body in the Lord. It is in the Eucharist that the real essence of the Church finds its expression. It is a community of believers who share in the life of the Risen Savior. They come together to celebrate the presence of the Lord. In this fraternal banquet, those who believe in Christ are all united together. Is it not striking that, in the early Church, the same word *communio* (communion) was used to designate both the act of receiving the Lord's Body and also the community of the faithful? The *Communio sancta* (Holy Communion = union with Christ) becomes the *communion sanctorum* (communion of saints). The fruit of communion is thus a constant and ever-deeper incorporation into the Body of Christ. It is important to note that even today we use one and the same phrase, "the Body of Christ," to designate both the sacred bread of the Eucharist and also the Church itself. Whoever receives the sacramental Body of the Lord is incorporated into the Mystical Body of Christ. "Because the loaf of bread is one, we, many though we are, are one body; for we all partake of the one loaf" (1 Cor 10:17).

5.5 Penance: friendship lives on forgiveness

5.5.0 "You shall seek the Lord, your God; and you shall indeed find him when you search after him with your whole heart and your whole soul. In your distress, when all these things shall have come upon you, you shall finally return to the Lord, your God, and heed his voice" (Dt 4:29-30).

"I will give them a new heart and put a new spirit within them; I will remove the stony heart from their bodies, and replace it with a natural heart, so that they will live according to my statutes, and observe and carry out my ordinances; thus they shall be my people and I will be their God" (Ezk 11:19-20).

5.5.1 Breach of faith. Throughout the Bible, there is a refrain of the "Lament of God's sorrow" over the alienation and infidelity of mankind. "It is your crimes that separate you from God" (Is 59:2).

Scripture repeats, in one context after another, what it really is to sin. Sin is infidelity to God, splitting with God. It dissolves the bonds of love between God and man. That is why the Old Testament describes it as a breach of covenant and as infidelity. In the final analysis, there is but one fundamental sin: rejecting God's love. That is the way that the very first sin is described. Ungrateful man turns aside from the God of love, and runs away.

But God remains faithful. Despite everything, he always presents an unqualified affirmation to man. On Golgotha, he pronounced this affirmation in an ultimate and decisive way.

5.5.2 "God is greater than our hearts" (1 Jn 3:20). "It is true that love is proved in fidelity, but it is fulfilled in forgiveness" (W. Bergengruen). Forgiving can bind a man in love even closer to his beloved. Friendship lives on forgiveness. Christ's call to confession and penance is the glad tidings of the fidelity and mercy of God. Repentance, in the Biblical sense of the word, is not primarily man's work. Even less is it something sad and sorrowful. God is waiting for the faithless sinner. He calls him, and offers him redemption. Doing penance means turning towards the Lord again, and entrusting oneself to him. "This is our way of knowing we are . . . at peace with him no matter what our consciences may charge us with; for God is greater than our hearts" (1 Jn 3:19-20). Penance is thus the encounter with a twofold love: the merciful love of God, and the repentant love of the sinner.

5.5.3 Reconciliation as gift and festival. "Turn back to me, says the Lord" (Zc 1:3). Turning back to God, that is what conversion is. Even the most sinful man can come home to his God. God's mercy always takes the initiative, and opens a way for the sinner into the joy and freedom of the children of God. Penance is thus, essentially, an offer to grace and happiness made to man by his loving God.

The full power to forgive sins was entrusted to his Church by the Risen Savior on Easter Day, as its greatest gift. Penance, accordingly, must ever be an event of joy and friendship! "Let us feast and celebrate" (Lk 15:23). Conversion leads to an encounter of love, and must ultimately merge into a stream of overflowing gratitude.

5.6 Prayer: lived friendship

5.6.0 Meeting with God, knowing and recognizing him—this is the theme of this chapter. Genuine friendship needs signs; it also needs words. Along with the sacraments, prayer is the most privileged means for meeting with God. Prayer is lived friendship with God.

Haste and activity, stress and the hectic pace of life, deadlines and pressures of every kind are the order of the day in our modern world. Those of our contemporaries who set some value on themselves all complain about this. One of our "contemporaries" appears to have thought and behaved differently. In a television sermon on Mark 1:12-15, Michel Quoist made some thought-provoking points:

> Jesus has all sorts of plans and objectives. He has got to go out and proclaim the Gospel of God. The Kingdom of God is near. He

does not have a single minute to lose. All humanity needs him. But it would appear that he managed his schedule very poorly and squandered his time.

First of all, he chose a poor time for his coming. He should have waited for the Concorde, so he could travel faster; for television, so he could speak to millions of people at one time; for the data bank, so that he could catalogue his members' cards and evaluate their test results and discover their needs, etc.

Secondly, he takes a lot of time before he starts upon his work. He starts out by spending thirty years in seclusion as a working man, who in absolutely no way at all could be said to stand out among his fellows, and who makes no effort at all to create or develop a special image for himself. And when he finally does get started speaking and being active, he is not yet sure of the means and methodology he should embark upon. He withdraws in order to spend long periods of silence praying to his Father. The Evangelists record a symbolic period of 40 days which he spends in the wilderness.

What a colossal waste of time! Simply unbelievable! It certainly looks as if there should be some other way to lead his life.

5.6.1 Seeking God's countenance. "As the hind longs for the running waters, so my soul longs for you, O God. Athirst is my soul for God, the living God. When shall I go and behold the face of God?" (Ps 42:2-3). "Of you my heart speaks; you my glance seeks; your presence, O Lord, I seek" (Ps 27:8). This expression, "seek the face of God," best describes what prayer was for the pious Israelite of the Old Testament: seeking God, being wholly in his presence. Prayer is a natural activity. According to the individual circumstances it can be a pleading and supplication, rejoicing and exultation, crying and laughing, complaining and grumbling, an obstinate wrangling or a blessed thanksgiving. Jesus, too, knew that he was very near to God the Father in every situation of his life. He sought out his face; he spoke intimately with him. He praised and begged and offered thanks.

5.6.2 Intimate familiarity with God. It would not be easy to describe in a single sentence just what Christian prayer really is. It would take a whole series of details, mosaic-like, to produce anything like a comprehensive picture. Just what is Christian prayer?

It is: a path into the depths of our own heart, to listen to God there; seeking out God's countenance in faith; coming into the presence of

God, to meet him in love; establishing contact with God; experiencing the closeness of God; simply being there in his presence; being poor and open and receptive to him; seeking the embrace of God; uniting oneself with him.

Christian prayer is thus an intimate familiarity with God "in Christ, with Christ and through Christ." It is a prayer in the name of Jesus. And this prayer has been promised its answer (Jn 14:13-14).

5.6.3 Expressing our love. Prayer is something profoundly human. It is not only a conversation about God, but an act of speaking with him. The heart of prayer is love. If I love someone, I cannot repress the thoughts of my heart. The words "I love you" rise unbidden to my lips. To my beloved, I can say everything. God, too, can listen. I can speak with him in every possible situation. Sickness and work, joy and misfortune, despair and hope—everything in human life can be the object of this dialogue with God. In the midst of my everyday living, with simple ejaculations or loving thoughts or with good intentions alone, I can seek to establish a rapid contact with God.

5.6.4 Putting love into words. Prayer is my life spread out before God. I can come into God's presence and show him what is moving me: my joys and my needs. This union with God frequently needs neither thoughts nor words. People in love can communicate with each other by a glance, by a smile, by a sigh. In the language of love, absolutely anything can work.

The body, too, is a means of contact. The first signs of tenderness are expressed in our hands and faces. In the most intensive encounters of love, the body loves together with the soul. Without a body, I am nowhere. Even in my meeting with God, the body can and must join the dialogue. Forming words, kneeling down, covering the face, folding the hands all are part and parcel of what we call prayer. Prayer is lived friendship with God.

5.6.5 Faith is something serious. For the believer, prayer is just as necessary and natural as the beating of the heart. If people in love never meet with each other, never speak with or think of each other, their love will soon dry up. The same thing happens to the believer if he does not pray: he withers and dies.

Like body and soul, like thought and word, prayer and faith are intimately connected with each other. Prayer is something very serious for the believer. If he does not pray, neither does he truly believe.

This experience of being close to God can, of course, never be the result of man's activity alone. Rather, it is fundamentally an offer on the part of God which man can only accept as a pure gift. The initiative does not come from man, but from God. It is God who speaks first. And my praying can only be an answer to the words that he has spoken first.

For many people, it is especially the prayer of petition that is the sum and substance of their faith. "Seek and you will find; ask and you will receive" (Mt 7:7). "Everything you ask the Father for in my name he will give you" (Jn 15:16; cf. Jn 14:13-14, 15:7, 16:24; Mt 7:7-11, 18:19, 21:22; Mk 11:24; Lk 11:9-13). These promises of Christ are for many people a stumbling block: "I have prayed and I have not been heard." This contradiction between the promise and their own experience is a source of concern for a lot of people, and for me, too. Perhaps Jesus' own behavior can show us in what direction the answer lies: "Take this cup away from me. But let it be as you would have it, not as I" (Mk 14:36). "When you pray, say: 'Our Father, who art in heaven . . .' " (Mt 6:9). After all, God is not a robot, simply producing the desired result in answer to a formula of prayer. Everything depends on whether or not I trust my Father God to love me and to do what is best for me. Does he not know better than I do, what is ultimately best suited for my welfare? Prayer of petition—sometimes a crisis of faith!

5.6.6 "Pray in the Holy Spirit" (Jude 20). The Spirit courts us from within. He cries in the heart of the believer: "Abba, dear father" (Gal 4:6). Christian prayer is a gift of the Holy Spirit (Rm 8:14-17, 26-27). "We do not know how to pray as we ought; but the Spirit himself makes intercession for us with groanings that cannot be expressed in speech" (Rm 8:26). The Holy Spirit as Author of Scripture (cf. 2 Tm 3:16), introduces the Bible-reader into a conversation with God, for "we address God whenever we pray; we hear him whenever we read the word of God" (St. Ambrose).

6. KNOWING AND RECOGNIZING GOD (GRATITUDE AND WITNESS)

6.0 Faith is friendship. Recognizing God's overpowering love and experiencing his closeness and his gifts, produces wonder and awe, trust and joy, praise and gratitude.

However, there is always the danger of striking a false note, of preaching a faith based only on emotion. Isn't our world sick? Doesn't even the believer have some unhappy experiences? Isn't our feeling towards life poisoned by sorrows and invaded by a sense of loathing? Isn't our present-day world a breeding ground for annoyance, anxiety and pessimism? Isn't it true that a person is part of the "in" group only if he can question everything and complain and accuse?

All this is very likely true. But must not we Christians place the accent more on the positive? Who is supposed to announce joy to the world, if we Christians do not do it? Christian faith means being surprised and being happy at the goodness of God. It means giving God due recognition for all he has done, and proclaiming his wonderful works before other men, even boasting about them. "How numerous have you made, O Lord, my God, your wondrous deeds! And in your plans for us there is none to equal you; should I wish to declare or to tell them, they would be too many to recount" (Ps 40:6).

6.1 Everything is faith

6.1.0 "It is owing to his favor that salvation is yours through faith. This is not your own doing, it is God's gift" (Ep 2:8).

For the men of our enlightened and technological age, the word "grace" has unfortunately become almost a foreign word. Man today wants to build and shape his own life. The only validity for him is what he himself can experience and accomplish, what he can control and regulate. Only when he comes against his ultimate limitations does he realize that he is prompted towards many things that he cannot accomplish by himself, and that he must rely upon what he has received as a gift.

Grace is the name we give to this element. It is not the product of our activity, our efforts, or our work, but rather is due solely to the love and initiative of God. At the outset, there is the invitation of God. That is why Christian faith is neither an inhuman experiment nor a "bounden duty," but a gift surpassing all our expectations. Love does not curtail a man's basic freedom, and Christian faith does not confine his initiative. The willingness to receive a gift from God and to be loved is what leads a man to joy and blessedness.

6.1.1 *"He has loved us first" (1 Jn 4:19)*. Redemption and faith are grace, unmerited love (Ep 2:8-9). The Gospel of Jesus Christ would be a counterfeit if we were to overlook this basic core of the glad tidings. "With age-old love I have loved you" (Jr 31:3). God turns to me in forgiveness, even when I am unfaithful to him and run away (Ezk 16; Ho 2). "Despite the increase of sin, grace has far surpassed it" (Rm 5:20). Again and again "God has visited his people" (Lk 7:16). The Easter Liturgy actually breaks out into a hyperbolic paean of praise: "O happy fault, to have deserved so great a Redeemer!"

6.1.2 *"I have chosen you" (Jn 15:16)*. Like a red thread, the theme of unmerited election runs through the entire Bible. From Abraham, through Moses and the Prophets, down to Mary and the Apostles it makes its way. "Before I formed you in the womb, I knew you" (Jr 1:5). God links his friendship and closeness with his free initiative and gift of love, by calling the chosen ones by name (Gn 15:1; Ex 3:4; 1 S 3:1-18), or by giving them a new name (Gn 17:5, 35:10; Mk 3:17). This election has only one basis: it is the result of love. "He has chosen you from all the nations on the face of the earth to be a people peculiarly his own. It was not because you are the largest of all nations that the Lord set his heart on you and chose you, for you are really the smallest of all nations. It was because the Lord loved you and because of his fidelity to the oath he had sworn to your fathers" (Dt 7:7-8).

6.1.3 *"God singled out the weak" (1 Cor 1:27)*. We live in a highly developed productive society. Almost everything today can be made or bought. To a large extent, all that counts is what a man owns or accomplishes or is able to do. These attitudes too easily transfer into the life of faith. Too many "devout Christians" lose courage when they see their own wretchedness, and recognize their own impotence, and have to admit that they cannot accomplish anything.

But here too, the message of the Bible is most consoling. Human weakness and divine strength are inseparably fused in the work of redemption. That is grace. "Man's poverty is the dwelling place, the vessel of divine power" (F.X. Durrwell). Christ himself was "crucified out of weakness, but he lives by the power of God" (2 Cor 13:4). Like a consistent theme, this thought runs through the whole history of salvation: "He singled out the weak of this world to shame the strong" (1 Cor 1:27). Moses, the young David, and Mary are a few examples. That is why in the New Testament it is precisely the poor and little who are declared blessed (Mt 5:3-5; Lk 1:51-53). They look to a salvation not resulting from their own power, but from God alone. They trust not in their earthly securities, but in the Lord alone. In the parable of the laborers in the vineyard (Mt 20:1-16), Christ goes so far as to promise "pay without work."

6.1.4 Theology of weakness. St. Paul, out of his own experience of impotence, has developed an entire "theology of weakness" (1 Cor 1:18-31, 2:1-5, 15:8-10; 2 Cor 3:4-5, 4:7-11, 11:16-33, 12:5-10). " '. . . in weakness power reaches perfection.' And so I willingly boast of my weaknesses instead, that the power of Christ may rest upon me. Therefore I am content with weakness, with mistreatment, with distress. . . . For when I am powerless, it is then that I am strong" (2 Cor 12:9-10).

St. Thérèse of the Child Jesus is a wonderful exemplar of this theology of weakness.

> My God, I am fortunate to feel little and weak before you; and my heart overflows with joy. God does not look so much at the bigness of our works, not even at the difficulties, but rather at the love with which we do them. So what do we have to fear? I truly feel that even if I had all the sins I could possibly commit on my conscience, I would go out, my heart broken with contrition, to throw myself into the arms of Jesus. I know how much he loves the lost child that comes back to him.

This attitude of being poor in the presence of God is a fundamental qualification for faith. This is not to say that man is meant to play the role of a dumb spectator in the story of salvation. He must work along with God, he must "work with anxious concern to achieve salvation" (Ph

2:12). There is no real contradiction between these two Biblical conceptions of man's proper role. They mutually complement each other, provided that we always put the accent in the right place.

6.2 Do not be afraid

6.2.0 Here is a group of men. They are all depressed, silent, moody. Often all it takes is for someone to come along, and immediately the whole atmosphere is changed.

Just such a scene is painted in the Gospel of St. John (Jn 20:19-20). A group of Jesus' friends are gathered in a room. For fear, they have locked all the doors. The disciples are discouraged and perplexed. They are mourning for their beloved master, who was crucified a few days earlier.

Then comes Christ, appearing in their midst. He shows them his hands and his side. "It is I. Do not be afraid." Suddenly, everything is different for these men. They are happy. In faith, they commit themselves to the friendly presence of Christ. And filled with awe, they tell St. Thomas: "We have seen the Lord."

Without Jesus Christ and his Spirit, the disciples are overcome with anxiety. They crowd together behind locked doors. But with Jesus comes peace, joy, and confidence in the future.

6.2.1 Why are you afraid? No one needs to be ashamed of his fears and anxieties. Every man experiences them. Isn't it comforting to know that even Jesus (Mk 14:32-36) and Mary (Lk 1:29-30) were afraid? Fear meets us in every conceivable form. Fear of some thing. Fear of some one. Fear lives in the hearts of many children, this bitter aftertaste of death: fear about going to school, fear about their parents and the future. Today, indeed, we are insured for everything and against everything. And still this fear, this anxiety, is a sickness of our modern times. Many people never do manage to overcome it. They are anxious to overcome it. They are anxious about everything: the past and the future, life and death. Many people's lives seem to consist of nothing but fear and anxiety.

Fear and anxiety are among the strongest emotions and experiences of human life. They are a mysterious mixture of a variety of mental and physical powers. The whole person is involved. On the one hand, fear can unleash unsuspected powers in a man. But on the other hand, it can hem him in, cripple him, make him sick, even drive him to suicide. Depression has become a popular sickness of our modern times. How can we overcome fear and anxiety? There are no patent solutions. Often, only a medical specialist can help. In certain cases, even he is powerless. What about "loving ourselves out" of our fears? Here is a recipe that can be prescribed to every child as he leaves the cradle.

6.2.2 Love yourself. Many people are severely shaken by life, and have never managed to face up to life's burdens. Many people carry within them a sort of undigested or unsubdued past: they are beset with inferiority complexes, and are not reconciled to their true selves. They do not recognize their own worth, and they despise themselves. These people either demean and ruin themselves, or they get intoxicated on their own ego, and thus find at least some confirmation of their own individuality.

"You shall love your neighbor as yourself" (Mt 19:19, 22:39; Rm 13:9; Gal 5:14; Jm 2:8). This first of all the commandments presupposes that I will love myself, that I may and indeed should love myself. But self-love is not an innate phenomenon. Love has to be learned. Self-love, too, is a lifelong objective. This friendly feeling in one's own heart is not such an easy matter. Loving myself means that I accept myself and my limitations, that I say "yes" to my own personality and that I be nice to myself. This is the way to build up my confidence in myself: I have a right to be me. I have a name and I should pronounce it with love. I have resolved to be exactly who I am. I love me, just as I am. I want to make peace with myself. I am the way I am, and I have a right to be that way. I look deep into myself, and reconcile myself with my life. I have the courage to be imperfect, and to face my own weaknesses. I do not need any self-pity. I can trust something to myself. I am going to be nice to myself. Faith is friendship.

In this willingness to accept self, there is an unexpected source of power. It is also the very basis for overcoming fear and anxiety. It is not worth the effort for me to try to justify myself, my ego, with all sorts of little tricks and lies. And God does not want his children to be soured on life. That is why the precept "Love yourself" is part of the very first commandment.

6.2.3 Long live patience and composure! "Fear not! Exult and rejoice! For the Lord has done great things" (Jl 2:21). Jesus demands a holy unconcern and detachment of his disciples: "Do not worry about your livelihood, what you are to eat or drink or use for clothing. Is not life more than food? Is not the body more valuable than clothes? Look at the birds in the sky. They do not sow nor reap, they gather nothing into barns; yet your heavenly Father feeds them. Are not you more important than they?" (Mt 6:25-26). This is not a cheap and easy Gospel. Quite the contrary. It amounts to nothing less than giving up our human securities and casting ourselves into the hands of God.

Why then is Christ's Church so beset with anxieties? And why are many Christians so depressed and so inclined to cower together behind locked doors? Why have so many of us become neurotic, preoccupied with crises? Why don't we allow ourselves more time and more peace of mind? Is the prayer "Rest in peace" valid only for our cemeteries? Where today are we to look for the unburdened happiness and serenity of the saints?

6.2.4 Sleep is Man's friend. "Indeed he neither slumbers nor sleeps, the guardian of Israel. . . . The Lord will guard your coming and your going, both now and forever" (Ps 121:4, 8). In our hectic age, many people suffer from sleeplessness. Faith is not, of course, a sleeping remedy. When the French poet Charles Péguy describes trust in God in images of idleness and sleep, all he means to say is what the poet of the Old Testament so magnificently described in Psalm 121.

> People who cannot sleep I cannot abide, says the Lord. Sleep is man's friend. Sleep is perhaps my most splendid creation. But now I hear that there are people who work well but sleep badly. Not to sleep. What a lack of trust in me. They hurt me. I take offense at them. A little. They put no trust in me. As the child nestles innocently in his mother's arms, just so they will not nestle innocently in the arms of my Providence. They have the courage and spirit to work. They do not have the courage to do nothing. To relax. To take a rest. To sleep. As if I were not capable of looking after their work for them for just a single night. As if I were not capable of perhaps worrying about it for a little while. Watching over it . . ." (Charles Péguy).

6.2.5 Have trust. Anxiety belongs to mankind. Christ, too, experienced anxiety: "My soul is sorrowful even to the point of dying." But still he trustingly committed himself into the hands of the One he called Father. "Father, into your hands I commend my spirit" (Lk 23:46). This was his dying prayer. And so, our Savior knows about human anxieties. He tries to offer his help. His message sounds like this: God has accepted man with all his crises and anxieties. "You will suffer in the world. But take courage. I have overcome the world" (Jn 16:33). "Do not let your hearts be troubled. Have faith in God and faith in me" (Jn 14:1). "Why are you so terrified? Why are you lacking in faith?" (Mk 4:40). For Christ, faith and trust are one and the same thing. In the original Greek text of the New Testament, the same word is used for both. Pope John XXIII used to speak very often on the subject of joyous trust and interior calm.

The true core of Christian faith is trust. But trust can be built only by experience. I am a believer only when I grasp how much I can build upon God's love and forgiveness. Christ did not reproach his friends for being weak and sinful, but for believing and trusting too little and for being too anxious. "Where is your courage? How little faith you have!" (Mt 8:26). "The man who believes does not tremble," Pope John used to say. This is not to say that it is enough to believe, and that then every form of anxiety will be banished. But still, trust and faith are the very best means for overcoming anxiety. God does not create anxiety—he wants to overcome it.

6.2.6 "I am with you" (Mt 28:20). "Do not be afraid!" We find this expression some 365 times in Holy Scripture. It is just as if I were meant to inscribe this motto onto every day of the year. What follows, as the reason why we are not to be afraid, is almost always the assurance: "It is I. I am with you."

Hardly anyone, when he is beset with anxiety, can set himself free without help time after time. We all need someone to help us. The frightened child runs to his mother. As soon as he is buried in her arms, the fear vanishes. Communication dissolves anxiety. And trust is always recognized as the force that dissolves it and sets free.

In the Old Testament, too, the believer is called to trust in God again and again. In the Psalms, we find men standing in the presence of God to express their need and anxiety. The Prophet Isaiah, for example, issues a constant invitation to trust. "God indeed is my savior; I am confident and unafraid. My strength and my courage is the Lord, and he has been my savior" (Is 12:2). "I have grasped you by the hand" (Is 42:6). "You shall call and the Lord will answer; you shall cry for help and he will say: Here I am!" (Is 58:9). "I will comfort you, as a child is comforted by his mother" (Is 66:13). "The Lord called me from birth, and from my mother's womb he gave me my name" (Is 49:1). "Can a mother forget her infant, be without tenderness for the child of her womb?" (Is 49:15).

But it is especially in the Gospel that we find the magnificent invitation to trust. For me, the ultimate basis for trusting is not some thing, but some one—the Risen Savior, who is with us to the end of time (Mt 28:20). In his presence, my anxieties and fears turn into blessedness. "Do not fear. . . . You have found favor with God" (Lk 1:30). Why is there so much fear and anxiety in the Church of Christ, and so little trust? Is there something wrong with our faith?

6.2.7 "Hope against hope" (cf. Rm 4:18). The Gospel of Christ is good tidings for those who live in the shadow of death. We Christians would have good reason to change the old proverb "Hope sustains a man" into a slightly different form: "Hope sustains the Christian." For "in hope we were saved" (Rm 8:24). For us, hope means a commitment to the Risen Savior, and thus also a commitment to the future. God is faithful. He stands by his promise. He will someday reveal the fullness of redemption to us. This must give us confidence. We must never despair, or bury our hope. "In you, O Lord, I take refuge; let me never be put to shame" (Ps 71:1). "Cast your care upon the Lord, and he will support you: never will he permit the just man to be disturbed" (Ps 55:23).

6.3 Wonder

6.3.0 "You great God, when I contemplate the world which you have created through your omnipotent word, my heart exults in you, great Ruler. How great you are! How great you are!" (Song of Hildor Janz). The ability to feel wonder is a precious gift for mankind. It is an interior answer to the unexpected and the incomprehensible. Wonder can be found already in our earliest childhood. The mother caresses her child, and he smiles his first smile. He looks in wonder at the burning candle, and speaks with the flowers. In his play, even the stones and sand are alive. Deeply stirred, he touches the beauties of creation. It is not in vain that we speak of the wondering eyes of the child, eyes that cannot tear themselves away from magic. In wonder, he leafs through the picture book of God. Like the saint or the artist, the child, in his blessed hours, looks quite through the surface of things. He sees into the very heart of things, where no other human eye can see and no other human ear can hear.

Unfortunately, too many grown-ups outgrow this wonder of childhood. In the film-oriented world of today, people are overwhelmed with pictures, flooded with impressions. And with the loss of wonder, we also outgrow our sense of reverence.

6.3.1 Perplexed. To love out of habit. To grow accustomed to love. How awful that sounds. Routine is the certain death of love. Wonder, on the other hand, is the opposite of taking something for granted, of the routine, of the trite and worn. By our sense of wonder, we humans can come into contact with the brink of eternity. Young lovers turn into children again. They see everything with new eyes. In the beloved, they always discover something new. They play tenderly with each other, and tease each other like children. And all this is far from childish.

This same sense of wonder is an important part of Christian faith. Faith means loving oneself and allowing oneself to accept a gift. That is why wonder is a fundamental Christian attitude, just like reverence. In the Psalms, the marvelous works of God are wondered at and praised. "It is good to give thanks to the Lord, to sing praise to your name, Most High. ... How great are your works, O Lord! How very deep are your thoughts" (Ps 92:2, 6).

6.3.2 "They were deeply shaken" (Ac 2:37). When God reveals himself, he accomplishes something unheard-of. He fills man with happiness and bliss. The Bible has many references to people who have been overpowered by wonder: "Nothing like this has ever been seen in Israel" (Mt 9:33). "They were struck with astonishment" (Ac 3:10). "They had all seen him and were terrified" (Mk 6:50). The women at the empty tomb were "half overjoyed, half fearful" (Mt 28:8). The disciples were frightened when they saw the Lord. "They were incredulous for sheer joy and wonder" (Lk 24:41). "Were not our hearts burning inside us as he talked to us on the road?" (Lk 24:32). When Jesus ascended into heaven, his disciples stood staring at the sky in fascination (Ac 1:10).

6.3.3 "They were incredulous" (Lk 24:41). Have we not managed to lose something of this Easter wonder? Or is the fact that God has loved us so much, something we just take for granted? The people in the Gospel feel a sense of wonder, and their hearts are moved. The sinners to whom Jesus brings his grace, the wondering children whom he enfolds in his arms, the sick whom he heals, all experience this. St. Paul, to whom the Risen Savior appeared, says in wonder: "Christ has loved me and delivered himself up for me" (Gal 2:20). "How deep are the riches and the wisdom and the knowledge of God! How inscrutable his judgments, how unsearchable his ways!" (Rm 11:33).

Many of the saints were perfect examples of how to be a child of God. For example, there is St. Francis, who expressed his great wonder of the world in his famous Canticle of the Sun.

The famous little note that Blaise Pascal had sewn into the lining of his coat records for us the moving experience of a "night of fire":

> Year of grace 1654. God of Abraham, God of Isaac, God of Jacob, not of the philosophers and scholars. Certainty, Certainty. Feel. Perceive. Joy. Peace. Forgetting the world and everything outside God. Only on the road that the Gospel teaches is he to be found. Grandeur of the human soul. Just Father, the world does not know you. But I know you. Joy. Joy. Joy. Tears of joy. . . .

You can just feel that in this experience of God, the heart is trembling and words fail.

6.4 Joy

6.4.0 "There is always far too little laughter. And that is mankind's greatest fault. . . . Christians would have to look a lot more redeemed to me before I could believe in their Redeemer." This reproach by Nietzsche must surely make us think.

My faith can be measured by whether or not I am happy with what Christ gives to me. As a Christian, I am supposed to be a "playing person," full of joy and trust.

In the Bible, from the first page to the last, glad tidings are proclaimed and joy is preached.

We can definitely call the Bible the best schoolbook of joy. For no book in the entire literature of the world contains the word and concept of joy as often as this book. I myself have catalogued these expressions. In all, there are about 2800 passages which speak of joy, gladness, cheerfulness, and happiness. Truly, this is glad tidings. God is joy and God wants to see us happy and God also has a sense of humor. If you really want to know what joy is, what it looks like, and how it is expressed, ask the Bible and think about what it says: health through joy (B. Pflüger).

"Rejoicing in the Lord must be your strength" (Ne 8:10). "I will be glad in the Lord" (Ps 104:34). "He has made everything appropriate to its time . . I recognized that there is nothing better than to be glad and to do well during life" (Ec 3:11-12). "Today is holy unto the Lord. Do not be sad, and do not weep" (Ne 8:9). "Rejoice! Again I say, Rejoice in the Lord!" (Ph 4:4). Laughter is not only healthful, it is also very Christian!

6.4.1 The gift of joy. The elders of the people went out to Samuel and asked him if he was bringing back good news or bad. "Good," he told them (1 S 16:4-5). Are we not also, for our world, the messengers and servants of joy?

The most noble and profound joy is not something that a man can make for himself. It has to be given to him. If I have the money, I can buy almost anything for myself today. But the joy that is to be found in a gift is not for sale, not even in the most comprehensive market in all the world. For behind the giving there is the loving person of the giver. In the present, someone is turning to me in love. They want to give me joy. If I see in a present only the thing that is given, and not the person who is giving it, then I have overlooked its most beautiful aspect.

The gift of joy is an inseparable part of Christian faith. If I were to rob the Gospel of its joy, I would be radically falsifying it. Christ turns to us human beings in love, and gives himself to us. "All this I tell you that my joy may be yours" (Jn 15:11; cf. Jn 16:24, 17:13).

The unsurpassable gift of God to us is not a precious thing, but a Person, whom we call Christ (Rm 8:32; 1 Cor 2:12; Jn 3:16). Faith is friendship making us happy!

Still, Christian joy is anything but a naive joy. As we have often pointed out, for the disciple of Christ there is only one way to eternal happiness, the way of the cross (Lk 9:23). Christ himself, during his life on earth, did not have only happy days. Most of the saints had to fight their way through sorrow and disillusionment, through dejection and pain. They often went through an experience of utter abandonment by God and a feeling of meaninglessness, before they arrived at a joy that was proved and purified in the cross.

6.4.2 Positive thinking. Whether I am young or old, there is one little bit of the world that I can change: my own heart. Everyone fills his heart with something. But not all of us with the same thing. Positive thinking leads to God, while negative thinking draws us away from him. The man who is always occupied with evil will come into contact with it over and over again. He lives in the ambience of evil and lets himself be influenced and infected by it. He forms closer and closer ties to it. He ends up worshipping evil. But the man who is happy, and thus enjoys the proximity of the good, comes into contact with God. When I am happy, then God is not far off; for God reveals himself in the power of joy.

6.4.3 Christian optimism. Why do people take so little time to work at being happy? So many of our contemporaries are afflicted with melancholy, gloom, pessimism and dejection. Despondency and bitterness fill their hearts. The heart without joy turns sick, and life becomes monotonous and tedious, desolate and empty. In the dead-end street of constant negation, a man becomes a sick despairer or an aggressive rebel.

If I put on dark glasses, then everything looks black, even white snow. I have to change glasses.

I photograph a young girl's laughing face. And the picture I develop shows a sneering and indistinct caricature. The adjustment was wrong. Proper adjustment is decisive.

You stare at your own shadow, and you do not see the sun anymore. Turn to face the sun. Then the shadows will dissipate behind you.

You are sitting at the table before a half-filled bottle. You can say that it is half empty, or you can say that it is half full. Each time you are right. You can be sad that half of it has already been drunk, or you can be happy that half of the bottle is still there. When the optimist and the pessimist see the same thing, they are not seeing the same thing.

"There is a song asleep in all things as they dream along, on and on; and the whole world starts to sing once you find the magic word" (Eichendorff). Cheerfulness brings magic to everything: the flowers start to talk and the animals start to laugh. Francis of Assisi certainly knew this. And folk wisdom is equally well-acquainted with it: a sense of humor spares you a psychiatrist. Lay down your heart in flowers, not in wrinkles. Joy is a loaf of bread that multiplies in the measure that it is cut and shared.

6.4.4 "Rejoice in the Lord" (Ph 4:4). Joy can only be experienced. Joy can be talked to death. Even a Gospel can be talked to death. Christ is not only someone to remember and an object of discussion; he is a living joy for me here and now. He has come "to preach the good news to the poor" (Lk 7:22). "As a bridegroom rejoices in his bride so shall your God rejoice in you" (Is 62:5). "There will be more joy in heaven over one repentant sinner than over ninety-nine righteous people who have no need to repent" (Lk 15:7).

The boldness of the Gospel extends to this "joy of the Lord."

My response to these glad tidings can only be a very intense joy. This Gospel joy is not a quiet and comfortable habit of life, but rather is an almost presumptuous trust in our Redeemer. "I know him in whom I have believed" (2 Tm 1:12). "I rejoice heartily in the Lord; in my God is the joy of my soul; for he has clothed me with a robe of salvation, and wrapped me in a mantle of justice. Like a bridegroom adorned with a diadem, like a bride bedecked with her jewels" (Is 61:10).

The real basis of Christian joy is Jesus Christ, and his Gospel which sets us free. Every encounter with Christ results in at least a quiet sense of joy. Mary carried Jesus in her womb and sang: "My being proclaims the greatness of the Lord" (Lk 1:46). The Shepherds at Bethlehem received the Christmas message: "You have nothing to fear. I come to proclaim good news to you" (Lk 2:10). The Apostles meet with the Risen Savior. "At the sight of the Lord, the disciples rejoiced" (Jn 20:20). Before his Ascension, Jesus took leave of his friends. "They returned to Jerusalem filled with joy" (Lk 24:52). They had a promise for later: "No one will take your joy away from you" (Jn 16:22).

6.5 The revolutionary Sermon on the Mount

6.5.0 St. Matthew (Mt 5:1-7:29) and St. Luke (Lk 6:17-49) record the so-called "Sermon on the Mount." This declaration of Jesus' program is the first sketch and the first model of Christianity. It is dynamite. Explosive power. It turns everything upside down and is little short of a revolution. Christ shows us the way to make our world of injustice and hate and brutality more human. And this sermon sets mankind upon the road to perfection.

6.5.1 The Beatitudes. The Sermon on the Mount begins with the "Beatitudes." In a few simple sentences, we hear all the motives and themes that constitute the essence of Christianity.

"Blessed are the poor in spirit." That means that all those who stand before God with empty hands can rejoice and trust in him to love and save them. God will show them how rich they are in his love.

"Blessed are the meek, the merciful, the peacemakers." This means that all who have turned their backs on violence, who neither oppress other men nor prey upon them, can rejoice. All those can rejoice who enlist their efforts in making people understand and accept and help and forgive one another. God will be just as good to them; in fact, much better. They will experience how closely they are united to God. They will live with him in a new world.

6.5.2 Blessed are you. . . . The weak and downtrodden were always Christ's first concern and passion. He calls those blessed who are poor and sorrowful.

Christ calls people blessed. He does not mean those who grasp greedily after transitory pleasures, or who scurry after the fleeting happiness found in power and possessions. He means those who are set free and redeemed. Blessedness is the calmness and the freedom from care of those who abandon themselves wholly to God. There is no other statement that sums up so clearly and so simply the Gospel's nature as the good news which evokes a sense of wonder and amazement, of joy and happiness. The Beatitudes are a fascinating song of hope. The outline sketch of Christianity they present is an unsurpassable parable of joy. It is one that we are meant to live right now.

6.5.3 The core of the Gospel. What have we made of these good tidings? Hasn't Christianity (at least as many people see it) become simply a system of beliefs to be taken for granted? Haven't we cast a shadow on this message of liberation and salvation, by weaving it into a network of precepts and laws and prohibitions and dogmas?

These Beatitudes are precisely what holds us back from the brink. They lead us back to the central focus. We Christians are expected to live much closer to the true core of the Gospel, and to declare our life program from that vantage point. In the Sermon on the Mount, Jesus Christ proclaims his Kingdom as a dwelling together in justice, freedom, peace, brotherhood and friendship. The Sermon on the Mount is designed to "engrave this Law in my innermost being" (cf. Ezk 36:26-27). If I have understood the proclamation of Jesus, then I must make every effort to be just as merciful, just as kind, just as patient and friendly as he is.

6.6 Gratitude

"Faith overflows into gratitude" (Col 2:7). A gift awakens joy in the receiver, and this develops into gratitude. Let my life be gratitude. Nobody can give the gift of life to himself. I can only accept it in gratitude. A loving gift from another person can wholly change a man. Love, too, no man can fabricate for himself. I can only receive it in gratitude. When all is said and done, I cannot acquire for myself the most important elements that contribute to my happiness. They must be given to me: life, love, and friendship.

Even the ability to believe is, in the last analysis, a gift. Believing means knowing that I have been given a gift from God and have been made happy by him. That is why I must confess with gratitude: "He has done great things for me: holy is his name" (Lk 1:49).

A Christian life must be one of gratitude. Thanks be to God for even the little everyday things: the murmur of the stream, the smile of a passer-by, our routine work. Thanks be to God above all else for Christ and his redemptive love. I cease being a Christian when I cease to give thanks. "Bless the Lord, O my soul; and all my being, bless his holy name. Bless the Lord, O my soul, and forget not all his benefits" (Ps 103:1-2). Let our whole life be a festival!

6.7 Festivity

Festivity belongs in our life. Man wants to celebrate his joy. He needs communally experienced joy. People invite each other to parties, and in a common happiness they get away from the everyday. The festival is a fleeting eternity. In festivity, time and eternity have managed to meet. In festivity, man tries to bring a small piece of heaven down to earth.

Christ has risen. He is alive. And it is he who turns our life into a constant festivity, even though cross and suffering still oppress us in the somber everyday of our living. Festivity is an expression of Christian hope: God will someday fulfill our life as festivity.

When Christians celebrate a festival, it is a community that celebrates, a community on its way. For "the Church marches along its pilgrim path between the persecution of the world and the consolations of God" (Augustine).

On this earth the singer must die; in heaven he will live forever. Here it is hope that lets him sing; there it will be gratification. Here it is the Alleluia of the man on his way; but there it is the Alleluia of the man at home. So sing and march along the way. What does it mean to march? Stride forward in the good. Sing and never miss your way, never take a step backwards, never stay in one place. Sing and march along (Augustine).

6.8 Testimony

6.8.0 Doors are symbols for so many events in our life. Doors can open, and they can close. Doors can unite, and they can divide. The Risen Savior passes through locked doors. He comes to see his frightened disciples in the room where they have locked themselves in, and everyone else out. And then suddenly, everything is changed. Their anxiety disappears. The Lord says to them: "As the Father has sent me, so I send you" (Jn 20:21). Then the doors are opened by the Apostles themselves. They go out into the world, because they have something and some One to proclaim to mankind. "Surely we cannot help speaking of what we have heard and seen" (Ac 4:20), Peter boldly confesses at his hearing before the High Council.

Christ does not want any free-loaders in his presence, not even religious ones. He sends out his followers with a mandate to mankind. He does not tell them to go out into the world and question everything, and turn everything upside down. He gives them this mandate: "Teach them . . . everything I have commanded you" (Mt 28:20). Out into the world of men—and out to Christ. For two thousand years, that has been the program of the Church. The Apostles were not comfortable functionaries in a comfortable church. They were restless men, who did not spare themselves, but expended all their strength in the service of the poorest and most abused. "The love of Christ impels us . . ." (2 Cor 5:14). "With power the apostles bore witness to the resurrection of the Lord Jesus" (Ac 4:33).

6.8.1 Convince. The man from whom Jesus had cast out a legion of demons wished to accompany him. "Jesus did not grant his request, but told him instead: 'Go home to your family and make it clear to them how much the Lord in his mercy has done for you.' At that the man went off and began to proclaim throughout the Ten Cities what Jesus had done for him. They were all amazed at what they heard" (Mk 5:19-20).

Union with Christ is never without its obligations. Christian faith means saying "Amen" to Christ, and admitting him into our hearts and confessing him. The happiness I experience as a gift is not something I can keep for myself. I have to tell it to others. "We are talking about what we know, and we are testifying to what we have seen" (cf. 1 Jn 1:1). Genuine testimony has to be convincing. This is of the essence. It must awaken faith in the other person as well. Conviction leads to witness. This is the way St. Paul became an Apostle, a Confessor of the faith. At his conversion, he heard these words: "I have appeared to you to designate you as my servant and as a witness to what you have seen of me and what you will see of me" (Ac 26:16). An experience of the closeness of God was given to St. Paul for the sake of his witnessing to Christ. And St. Paul did indeed become a witness and confess. "Because I believed, I spoke out" (2 Cor 4:13). "I determined that . . . I would speak of nothing but Christ, and him crucified" (1 Cor 2:2). "Never be ashamed of your testimony to the Lord" (2 Tm 1:8). A non-missionary Church is a demissionized Church!

6.8.2 "Practicing" Christians. When a person no longer goes to Mass on Sunday, we say that he is no longer "practicing." Some people are inclined to say: "Some practicing Christians are worse. On Sunday they eat the Body of the Lord in Church, and during the week they bite the brothers of the Lord. I prefer not to go to Church on Sunday, but I live like a Christian during the week!" This either-or policy is really not applicable here. "Practicing" means both. Show your faith to Christ—show your faith to man.

6.8.3 Come—go. "He . . . summoned the men he himself had decided on, who came and joined him . . . whom he would send to preach the good news" (Mk 3:13-14). "Come" (Mt 4:19). "Go" (Mt 28:19). Come—go. That is how God speaks to his favorites (cf. Gn 12:1). This twofold mission of the Christian—oriented towards both God and man—is the mystery of the Christian apostolate. The closer someone is united with Christ, the closer he must be with men. We are "a chosen race, a royal priesthood, a holy nation, a people he claims for his own to proclaim the glorious works" of God (1 P 2:9).

6.8.4 Faith and life. Faith and life have to overlap. They must never shut each other out. It is from faith that the impulses must come that will have a bearing on the real questions and experiences of men today. The Gospel does not speak of any bargain-basement Christianity. I cannot forget my faith in the umbrella stand at Church. I cannot leave God simply "lying there" in the Church; I have to take him out into my everyday life. My faith must determine my entire existence—from money matters all the way to walking in a dear friend's funeral procession.

In Chapter 11 of the Letter to the Hebrews, we are presented with various figures of faith. Faith has determined the entire life of these men. We too are met by God in the midst of our life. We recognize his will not, at first, in some direct divine inspiration, but in the events of our concrete everyday living.

6.8.5 Faith in the everyday. Once there were two monks who each read in an old book that there was, at the end of the earth, a place where heaven and earth met. They decided to go out and look for it, and not to come back until they had found it. They traveled all over the world, encountered perils beyond counting, suffered all the privations that a trip around the world demands, and all the temptations that could ever turn a man aside from his goal. There was a door there, they had read, and you only needed to knock on it and you would find yourself in the presence of God. Finally, they found what they were looking for. They knocked on the door. With trembling hearts they watched it slowly open, and when they went inside they were standing back home in their monastery cells. Then they began to understand. The place where heaven and earth meet is to be found in our everyday lives, in the place where God has appointed us to be (Legend retold by Jorg Zink).

6.8.6 Stop the world; I want to get off. Martyrs are also called blood-witnesses. Martyrdom is a radical predilection for Christ. "We drink Christ's Blood so that we can shed our own blood for him" (Cyprian). Even for the Christian, faith does not resolve every question. In his imitation of Christ, he can still live with unsolved questions. Even the Christian's life is largely a way of the cross. Jesus did not promise his friends happiness, and freedom from suffering in this world. On the contrary, he has methods all his own. He calls his friends to follow his own way of the cross. "If a man wishes to come after me, he must deny his very self, take up his cross, and begin to follow in my footsteps" (Mt 16:24). Even in our "insane world of today," there are a great number of people who are tired of living. It takes courage to live. "In earlier times, they used to call martyrs people who had the courage to give up their life out of love for Christ. Today, they ought to call martyrs people who have the courage to live on in joy and gratitude out of love for Christ" (F.X. Durrwell).

6.9 The missionary call

6.9.0 Real love has to be active love. The Gospel of Matthew closes with our Lord's missionary mandate:

> At the sight of him, those who had entertained doubts fell down in homage. Jesus came forward and addressed them in these words: "Full authority has been given to me both in heaven and on earth; go, therefore, and make disciples of all the nations. Baptize them in the name of the Father and of the Son and of the Holy Spirit. Teach them to carry out everything I have commanded you. And know that I am with you always, until the end of the world!" (Mt 28:17-20).

6.9.1 Redemption: all-embracing salvation of mankind. Redemption, liberation, salvation! These three words express what Christ and his Gospel really mean. Christ is our salvation and our Savior. It is obvious that our Savior was concerned with setting man free from sin and godlessness, and redeeming him and leading him to God. But the unholy network of evil, in whose toils man has been caught up, enfolds the human heart and human society. So many things hem us in, and reduce our freedom. Anxieties and inner inhibitions of every kind can enslave us. Economic pressures clutch at many of our contemporaries from every side: they are preyed upon, impoverished, and driven headlong into misery. Social and political pressures rob so many people of their freedom. They are humiliated in every way, only to end up in the torture chambers, in the concentration camps, and in the gas chambers. Redemption, in the last analysis, is aimed at the total, all-encompassing liberation of mankind. It is a question of saving man, of making the whole man whole.

6.9.2 We are God's ultimate proclamation. Christ has no hands of his own, only our hands, to do his work today. He has no feet of his own, only our feet, to lead men along his way. Christ has no lips of his own, only our lips, to tell men about him. He has no help, only your help, to bring men over to his side. We are the only Bible that the public still reads. We are God's final proclamation, written in deeds, and words. And if the writing is falsified, if it cannot be read? If our hands are busy with other things than his? If our feet go off into the paths of sin? If our lips speak what he would have rejected? Are we hoping to be able to serve him, without imitating him? (14th cent.).

6.9.3 Our concern: man. God's concern is man, and our concern is man. To free man, to give him well-being on earth and ultimate salvation—that was the whole objective of Christ's life. Shortly before his death, he gave his disciples a new commandment: "Love one another, as I have loved you" (Jn 15:12). Upon taking leave of his followers, he said: "Go into the whole world and proclaim the good news to all creation" (Mk 16:15). Christ's friends are supposed to continue his work on earth.

Jesus is concerned with the all-embracing welfare of the whole man. This concern is frequently divided in pieces today, sometimes violently. One group says that mission means announcing the Gospel, with the objective of converting non-Christians to the Christian faith. They base their interpretation upon Christ's missionary mandate (Mt 28:18-20). Another group says that mission is service to mankind with the objective of universally promoting and realizing the potential of human life: mission is humanization. They, for their part, argue from the great commandment to love one's neighbor (Mt 22:39; cf. Lk 10:25-37; Mt 25:31-46). Proclamation or service, conversion or humanization—these are the slogans that characterize the two directions.

"Proclamation of the Gospel and aid to human development are indeed to be clearly differentiated between; but still they are inseparably bound up with each other." This significant statement of Pope John Paul II stresses the fact that Christ's mandate is indivisible, and that the mission of the Church is to be confined to neither one realm nor the other. Our concern is man and his universal welfare. Faith is friendship!

6.9.4 Still pagans to convert? Many modern prophets say that we should let the pagans exist in the faith they have. Conversion is intolerance and arrogance. But we must reply: "It is not ourselves we preach but Christ Jesus as Lord" (2 Cor 4:5). "Woe to me if I do not preach the Gospel" (1 Cor 9:16). That is what St. Paul writes, the Apostle to the Gentiles.

Preaching the Gospel means confessing Jesus Christ. Why is it so necessary to confess this person above all others? Michel Quoist tries to give a clear and simple answer to this question:

> I personally have found the answer on the basis of a painful and at the same time very beautiful experience. An acquaintance of mine had her child interned in a concentration camp during the war, when he was only an infant. Later, they learned that the child was alive. He had grown to a man. They looked for him, and finally managed to find him. His mother told me later how hard it was for them to meet each other again. She sat there overcome with

emotion while he knelt before her and touched her face with trembling fingers, and kept saying "You are my mother! You are my mother!" Then all of a sudden, she realized what was happening. This young man had been her son for about twenty years. He had everything he had, only because she had given him the gift of life. But at the same time he had nothing, because he did not know from whom he had received this gift of life, did not even know his mother's face or name. And thus, he was not able to pass on in perfect awareness the love that she had shown him. If there were even one single man on earth who did not know Jesus Christ, and if this man were already living in Christ's life because he loved his fellow-man, we would still, nonetheless, have to do everything we could to bring him to an encounter with Jesus and to a full knowledge of him. For it is a wonderful thing to be alive, and it is a wonderful thing to be saved, and it is a wonderful thing to be loved—but it is all a tragically fragmentary experience so long as we do not know whom we are to thank for everything.

6.9.5 For everyone—a life worthy of a human person. Jesus had a special leaning towards the poor. This great portion of humanity, however, is condemned in our modern world beyond hope. And not infrequently, a rich Church lives in a world of starving people.

Christian missionary activity also means service and aid for development. The man who confesses his adherence to Christ must work for world-wide social justice, for the liberating development of all peoples, for a worthy life for everyone. The object of this development is man himself. At this point, we touch upon a vital nerve of Christianity. Christ proclaimed the good tidings to the poor. He freed the enslaved. He brought hope to the world (1 P 1:3-5). For him, this was the full range of mission.

Our service must incorporate the following objectives:
a. To free mankind from hunger, poverty and oppression. The most basic needs have precedence: sufficient nourishment, healthy living conditions, a suitable level of provision for health and education. This means war on disease, oppression, discrimination, illiteracy and human misery.
b. To give people the potential for taking responsibility in personal life and in community life. The key-words here are partnership, solidarity, and aid to self-help. At the same time, we must try to curb our tendency to practice a sort of paternalism. We must not turn aid into a business.
c. To give them the potential to develop their own cultural individuality. Christ is not allied to any single culture. Mission activity must never set

out to destroy; it must accept the values current in that society and respect "what is in every man" (Jn 2:25).
d. To give them the potential to participate as fully qualified citizens in the life of humanity as a whole. Every man is a citizen of this world, and a member of human society.

PART TWO:

CHRISTIAN FAITH IS ORIENTED TOWARDS COMMUNITY

7. FRATERNAL FAITH

7.0 The world is growing smaller. We have turned into neighbors of each other. On the one hand, modern man feels a loneliness that has hardly ever been felt before. And on the other hand, he is tortured by an insatiable hunger for his fellow man, for solidarity, for love and peace, for brotherhood and community. On the one hand, humanity is split into two gigantic blocs of rich and poor. The armed super-powers of East and West oppose each other. But on the other hand, people are drawing together. Vacation tours and news satellites draw us closer and closer together. The modern means of transportation and communication, the mass media and space flights make the inhabitants of this globe more and more into neighbors, into one family with but a single destiny.

The American Apollo program was a large-scale demonstration of cooperation. In some 20,000 separate occupations and places of work, more than 300,000 people all worked together. We are the first generation to have consciously experienced the fact that all mankind is a single unity. All of us are together in the one great game of world history.

Mankind today looks for a community. Perhaps this is a new demand upon our Christian faith.

7.1 We believe

I believe! These are the beginning words of the Apostles' Creed. This Credo developed from the early Baptismal liturgy. It was a personal answer to the question: "Do you believe?" "Credo. I believe." I am I. And I have a name. Even in the presence of God, I stand as a unique mystery. He speaks to me personally. I believe. In this, I cannot substitute anyone else for myself. Faith is a personal and free acceptance of the good tidings; it is a conversion, a turning (as the Latin word *conversio* suggests) to the loving Person of God; a trusting surrender to the God of Abraham and Isaac and Jacob; an encounter with our Lord Jesus Christ. Faith is friendship.

We believe; we confess; we look forward. This is the substance of our prayer in the Great Creed of the Council of Nicaea, the result of a community effort to establish the standard statement of Christian belief. My personal credo must correspond with the official Creed of the Church. My personal confession of faith must, where necessary, be corrected by what the community of the faithful confesses. Christian faith is genuine only when it is oriented towards the community, both ecclesial and fraternal. The figures of the brother and the sister always stand in the center of Christianity. Christian faith is conceived and nourished in the community, and it is geared towards the community. Faith is friendship!

7.2 Credo as symbol

In our Credo, the knowledge and experience of faith enjoyed by several generations of Christians is summed up. The basic formula of this confession of faith was worked out in the second and third centuries, in connection with the Baptismal ceremony. The Christians took great pains to express what they believed in words, in order to pass it on without falsification from one generation to the other. In those days, they called the Creed *symbolum*. This word comes from the Greek word *symballein*, and means "to put something together." Earlier, two connectable pieces of a ring or a staff served as tokens of identification for guest-friends, for heralds or the parties to a covenant.

Christian faith demands unity, and is oriented towards a church. Every individual in the early Church held the faith in his own hands like an imperfect piece that could find its authenticity and totality only in proper connection with the faith of all the others.

7.3 Christ our brother

Brother! This is a core word in our faith. In Christ, God has become our brother. One of us. The Incarnate God came with his human body, which was exactly like ours. He was a friend of the little people, the sorrowing, the wronged, the downtrodden. He was born into a situation of fear and anxiety, as St. Matthew reports it. He did not die in his bed. He was crucified and tortured. In his death, he cried the cry of final desolation. At the beginning was the manger, at the end the cross. God became our Brother.

Since that time, the figure of the brother has always been close to the heart of Christianity. Our faith is a fraternal faith. Our brother (or sister) is the privileged place for meeting with God. "I assure you, as often as you did it for one of my least brothers, you did it for me" (Mt 25:40).

7.4 A people of believers

7.4.0 The Church is not a closed, static community. Here below, it is constantly on its way and is always growing. The Second Vatican Council seems particularly fond of the expression "the wandering people of God, the pilgrim Church." Church, that is us: people of flesh and blood. The Church is on a pilgrimage through this world and through time. Her real story is what she writes into the history of humanity.

This wandering people is a people of believers. It possesses the word of God, the Spirit of Truth and the promise of our Lord. And it knows the direction to follow. Still, it has to seek out its way into the future. It must painstakingly follow out the way of faith, and stride onward into uncertainty and hazard. We must not try to conceal the misery of the Church. But her real grandeur, and her whole core and being, is Christ the Lord.

7.4.1 *Church: belonging to the Lord*. The English word "church" comes from the Greek word *kyriakē (oikia)*, "Lord's (house)." It suggests that this people belongs to the crucified and risen Savior. The Church can never make herself into her own purpose or objective. She remains the Church only so long as she refers herself and everything else to Christ.

We also call the Church by other names: the Body of Christ, the Bride of Christ. These names unmistakably express her intimate union with the Lord. Christ calls us "my disciples, my friends, my people, mine." We, for our part, call him "our Lord." "So too we, though many, are one body in Christ and individually members one of another" (Rm 12:5). We can be Christians only by a very close adherence to Christ. Loving Christ means loving him together with his whole Body, the Church (1 Cor 6:15, 10:16-17, 12:12-27; Ep 1:22-23, 4:3-6; Col 1:24, 3:15).

7.4.2 "I have called you friends" (Jn 15:15). This friendly relationship between the Lord and the community of the faithful was frequently pointed out by Christ. Let us recall a few words from the New Testament: "There is no greater love than this: to lay down one's life for one's friends" (Jn 15:13). "He had loved his own in this world, and would show his love for them to the end" (Jn 13:1).

To them he entrusts everything, even his own self, his body: "Take and eat; this is my body" (Mt 26:26). His spirit: "The Spirit of truth . . . will be within you" (Jn 14:17). His word: "If you live in me, and my words stay part of you, you may ask what you will—it will be done for you" (Jn 15:7). His commandment: "A new commandment I give to you. This is my commandment: Love one another" (Jn 15:12). His mandate: "Go and make disciples of all the nations" (Mt 28:19). He promises in return that he will be close at hand: "Know that I am with you always, until the end of the world" (Mt 28:20).

These few characteristic words are enough to prove that we cannot separate Christ from his Church. Without the Church, none of us would know who Christ is. Without the Church, there would be no Gospel and no sacraments. Christ without the Church would no longer be the Christ of our faith. The Church, for her part, must constantly strive to remain an unadulterated sign of the presence of Christ. She must continue to tell mankind about the history of God, and continue to live it.

7.5 Faith: conceived in community

7.5.0 Human life is entrusted to a community. God said to our first parents: "Increase and multiply" (Gn 1:28). Since that time, human life has flowed down through the centuries from one womb to another. A community of generations. Man and woman love each other, and thus the gift of life is passed on. The individual is born out of the community. The child is born into a family, and thereby also into the greater family of all humanity. Community of love and community of life.

7.5.1 Mother Church. The believer also comes from a community. Our faith is not the result of solitary meditation. It comes from the witness of other people. It comes from listening and from answers, from receiving and giving.

The Church is that fraternal community which gives us our faith. She is our mother. "On her lap I learned everything" (Paul Claudel). Faith is conceived in the community. Generally, the parents are the first pastors and catechists of their children. When an expectant mother prays or takes communion, perhaps even then, in some mysterious way, the very first seeds of faith sink into the tender soul of her child. Perhaps it is already then that she gives him a capacity for faith. In youthful or adult years, a contact with a thoroughly convinced believer or a missionary preacher can serve to awaken faith.

7.5.2 Baptism: birth and enlightenment. Baptism is a birth into a new life. We are "begotten of water and Spirit" (Jn 3:5). In earlier times Baptism was called *illuminatio* (enlightenment), and baptized Christians were called "seers." In Baptism, we learn to know and recognize Christ. In the baptismal ceremonies, we are shown with remarkable drama how faith comes from the community and is conceived in community. Faith and baptism are essentially geared for each other.

The baptismal rite begins with two questions: What is the child's name? What do you ask of the Church? The answers to the second question are significant: "faith" or "eternal life" or "acceptance into the Church." Everyone has his own name. It is unique. Faith and acceptance into the Church are given to him by the community of the faithful.

Then the person to be baptized is led into the house of God, in the midst of the assembled faithful. Before the ceremony, the Creed is prayed; then the faith of the candidate for Baptism must correspond to the faith of the Church.

7.6 Faith: nourished in the community

7.6.0 Faith is life. Faith and Baptism belong together. But faith is much like human life. In order for it to grow, the fertilized egg (embryo) must find a place to rest in the mother's womb. In like manner, the young, embryonic faith and the new life conceived in Baptism need a place to rest within the womb of Mother Church. There, the warmth of fraternal love must protect and nourish and let it grow.

7.6.1 Mutual edification. Our faith is the faith of the pilgrim—a searching, questioning, troubling and struggling faith. Faith is never easy; but the problems facing it today seem to be greater than ever before. Fraternal faith means that we help each other to overcome these crises of belief. We must bear with the problems others have in believing.

"As members of one body you have been called" (Col 3:15). "For I long to see you and share with you some spiritual gift to strengthen you—rather, what I wish is that we may be mutually encouraged by our common faith" (Rm 1:11-12).

Christian faith is a living mutual relationship, a lived exchange of trust between the individual and the community. Everyone can strengthen their neighbor in faith, can support and help him along. But we also need our neighbor to mature and grow in our own faith. One example among many is the meeting between two women, Mary and Elizabeth (Lk 39:56). Elizabeth says: "Blest is she who trusted. . . ." She shares Mary's faith. Mary, for her part, confirms her faith in the presence of her cousin when she intones a glad song of praise: "My being proclaims the greatness of the Lord." Mary and Elizabeth strengthen each other in their faith. They thus function for each other as "good administrators of the manifold grace of God" (1 P 4:10).

7.6.2 Partners in faith and marriage. Nowadays many marriages are threatened. Something in them has gone fundamentally wrong. In many Christian marriages, faith no longer has any role to play at all. Many spouses part company at the drop of a hat. Is marriage only a miserable experiment? For Christians, at least, it certainly should not be. Shouldn't we rather make an increased effort to discover the innermost essence and mandate of the sacrament of marriage? In Christian marriage, two baptized and believing people are consecrated to each other. That is why we call marriage a sacrament. Husband and wife are supposed to be each other's partner in faith. Neither of the two can make their own way to God, or go to heaven alone. Each of them is oriented towards the other. Each becomes, for the other, a priestly dispenser of divine grace.

It is a primary duty of Christian married couples to accompany each other in their faith, to mutually sanctify each other in a living exchange of faith. On the day of their wedding, they confer upon each other the sacrament of marriage. Each partner is a pastor for the other. As comrades in faith, they will be together for their whole life long, on the way towards God.

Love can last forever. That is the great promise of Christian marriage: our marriage is our communal path to heaven. We are each other's guides along the way. We bear responsibility for each other. We hope to be together one day with Christ. Companions in life—companions in heaven—companions in eternity!

Sacraments are signs of faith. The sacrament of marriage, as long as it lasts, is oriented towards faith. But what if faith weakens in the marriage partners, if faith dies away? Can we still speak of a sacrament in their marriage?

7.6.3 Bringing up children is a pastoral care. Parents are the destined guardians of both their children and their children's faith. After the Baptism of their child, they are charged with bringing up a person who is also a child of God. Bringing up children means helping them to develop in faith, as well. Father and mother are the very first instructors in the faith. Long before their children receive any formal instruction in religion, the parents are already teaching them by word and example. The mother's role, especially, can never be appreciated highly enough. She is truly a pastor for her child when she teaches him to make the sign of the cross, to fold his hands, to say his first prayers.

The Second Vatican Council calls the family "a sort of home Church," a kind of "micro-Church." St. Augustine refers to fathers as fellow-bishops and heads of this miniature Church: "You, fathers, represent me; you take my place. Everyone who is head of a family must exercise the office of bishop, and be responsible for the faith of his charges."

7.6.4 Preaching: faith comes from hearing. Faith means accepting the good news of Christ which is announced to us through the Church. The genuine proclamation of the faith is always a call to belief. "Faith comes from hearing" (Rm 10:17).

The man who preaches has to testify to what he himself believes as a member of the community of faith. Testimony and confession make the preaching. That is why his credo must totally agree with the credo of the Church.

When a person gives testimony through his preaching to strengthen others in their faith, he will see that the whole assembled congregation, for its part, supports his own faith. Preaching the word of God amounts to a mutual exchange of the experiences and convictions of faith.

7.6.5 Liturgy and Eucharist: service of faith. Finally, the liturgy is a fraternal service in faith and for faith. What the community, in its faith, celebrates in faith, is meant to nourish and mature the faith of each individual member.

The Eucharist is the one great "mystery of faith." The faithful eat one and the same bread at one and the same table, and thereby communally bind themselves together in the Lord. The celebration is a mutual exchange and dialogue between the brethren in the faith. Each individual is, at the same time, both giver and receiver. In the formula of greeting, "The Lord be with you—and also with you," the faithful wish the gift of the Lord upon each other. In the confession of guilt, each individual admits that he is a sinner and prays for his sinful fellow Christians. The very ritual of confession thus becomes a call to conversion and to deeper faith. The preface is an encouragement to raise our hearts to God: in this dialogue we all invite each other to faith. In the fraternal meal that follows, the communicant receives the "mystery of faith." In this bread of unity, his faith is nourished.

7.7 Faith: community oriented

7.7.0 O Lord Jesus Christ, you were born of a Hebrew mother, you were filled with joy at the faith of a Syrian woman and a Roman soldier, you received in friendship the Greeks who came looking for you, you permitted an African to carry your cross with you—help us to bring together men of every race as fellow heirs into your kingdom. Amen. (African prayer).

7.7.1 *Knowledge of the saints*. Then love provided me with a basic viewpoint for my vocation. I saw that the body of the Church is made up of different kinds of limbs and members. I saw that the Church has a heart and that this heart is burning with love. I was able to see that this one love stirs all the members of the Church to activity, that no apostles would ever again preach the Gospel and no martyrs would ever again shed their blood if this love died out. I beheld and recognized that this love encompasses every vocation in itself, that this love is everything. Then my heart was intoxicated with supreme joy. Then I cried out: Jesus, my love, finally I have found my vocation. My vocation is love! I have found my place in the Church. You have given it to me, my God. In the heart of the Church, my mother, I will be a messenger of Love. And thus I will be everything, and my great longing will be stilled (St. Thérèse of Lisieux).

7.7.2 *Christian faith is Church faith*. Faith is friendship. Thus it consists of a whole network of friendly relationships toward Christ and his Church. Christian faith deserves this name only when it is community-oriented and open to our brother. That is, only when it is a Church faith. A Christian who attacks the unity of the Church is really biting his own flesh. That is why Christ commanded his Apostles, shortly before his death, to be one, "so that the world will believe" (Jn 17:21). "Have a passionate desire for the unity of the body of Christ" (Rule of Taizé).

The unity of the Body of Christ does not, however, imply uniformity and sterile imitation. Individuality in unity, and unity in multiformity! Multiplicity in peoples, races and cultures; in offices and services; in rites and practices; of bishoprics and Eastern Churches. One of the greatest temptations that has faced the Church from time immemorial has been the threat of centralism and imitation, impatience and intolerance.

Our faith can, and must, be a critical faith. It is true that the Church has, in the course of time, accomplished great things. Still, we must not simply justify everything that Christians and the leaders of our Church have done over the course of the centuries. Many things were wrong. And we must honestly admit the mistakes. What was wrong cannot simply be exonerated. We suffer today under the burden of a Church history that is partially laden with guilt. Who could possibly deny this fact?

Still, annoyance with the Church is anything but a healthy sign for the faith of the Christian. We can know and understand anyone—even God (1 Jn 4:8)—only in love. And thus, we shall understand the Church only when we are bound to her in ties of friendship, when we really love her the way a man loves his own mother. For the Church is truly our mother—and our cross! The faith of the individual is divided against itself whenever it is in open or secret contradiction to the essential fund of faith proclaimed by the Church. "The sign of unity is worth much more than even the most outstanding individual accomplishment" (Roger Schutz). In our age of confusion, we would be very well advised to fall back upon this basic truth. Schisms in the faith, as well as attempts at genuine ecumenism, always begin in the innermost hearts of the people of God.

7.7.3 Ecumenism. "Be one, so that the world will believe" (Jn 17:21). The people of God are in a state of fragmentation. The splits among Christians are a scandal. Christianity is losing its credibility. Might we not characterize the newly-awakened longing for unity as the Holy Spirit's special gift to our century?

Basic Position of Fidelity: "Every renewal in the Church consists essentially in the growth of fidelity to the Church's own call" (Second Vatican Council). We can renew the Body of Christ in its proper unity only from within, never by further fragmenting it. Ecumenism, accordingly, does not consist simply in glossing over the differences between the various Churches, nor in denying these differences in practice, nor in acting as if the Christian Churches had already recovered their full and perfect unity.

Basic Position of Openness: The true ecumenical spirit consists in the wish and the will to learn to know each other, mutually and without prejudices. It aims to accentuate those areas which we have in common and which already serve to unite us, so as to foster a reciprocal respect for everything that still keeps us apart. The object is to work enthusiastically for everything which can further the reconciliation and unity of the different confessions (from common prayer to pastoral and social cooperation). Faith is friendship!

But the very first principle of any genuine ecumenism always consists in this truth: we can approach each other only to the degree that we communally approach the Lord. It is like a pyramid, in which the distance between the two sides grows less and less, the closer we come to the top.

7.7.4 Solidarity: we are all brothers. Jesus willed to establish a community of brothers and sisters. He himself practiced solidarity not only with his friends, but also with the poor and the exploited, with sinners and prostitutes, with publicans (tax-collectors) and outsiders, with those who were despised on religious or political grounds, with the failures and the rejects, with the lepers and the lame and the blind.

Imitating Christ, the Church must set up the standard of hope, and proclaim her solidarity with the suffering, the oppressed, and the sinful. Neither the individual Christian nor the Church can dare to close in on themselves, and become an island. The Christianity of self-preservation must more and more become a Christianity of radiation. It must enter into dialogue with the world of today—and that includes the Third World! "The joy and hope, oppression and suffering of modern man, especially the poor and oppressed of every kind, are at the same time the joy and hope, oppression and suffering of Christ's disciples. And there is nothing truly human that does not find its echo in their heart" (Second Vatican Council). This must not be merely a pious wish—it must become more and more the program of the Church's activity in the world.

7.7.5 Love of foreigners or love of neighbor? Let me recount the story of my friend Carl. He was a mountain man, and lived in constant hostility towards the neighbors with whom he shared his meadow. Many a time, I had to act as mediator and smooth things over. One weekend, I ran into Carl and asked him where he'd been. "Oh," he answered enthusiastically, "You should have been there! We had a big demonstration in North Park!" "A demonstration? What was it about?" "We were protesting the exploitation of the Coolies in Shanghai." "Goodness, gracious!" I exclaimed, "The Coolies in Shanghai! Are you interested in something that far away?" "Yes indeed," Carl answered, "We are pledged to solidarity with them. Complete solidarity! Everyone is our brother." You could still sense the fire of that splendid demonstration. "Everyone is your brother," I said happily, "O Carl! Then tonight you can go over to your neighbor's and call him brother." At that, the radiance disappeared from his face. He took on a grim expression. "What? That lout? That good-for-nothing? That. . . . Just let me tell you what he did yesterday. . . . But I'll get even with him all right. . . ." "So everyone is our brother," I thought as I turned to go (Wilhelm Busch).

7.7.6 Love one another. One day, the bishop came to visit a small village school. He asked one of the classes what the language of the Church was. A small child, who had never even heard of the word "Latin," answered without a moment's hesitation: "The language of the Church is love." If Jesus had been there, he would have smiled and rejoiced. "Father, I thank you for having revealed these things to the little ones" (Mt 11:25). But whether the language of Christians has really always been love—that is a very different matter.

Love. Love of neighbor. That is the fundamental concept of Christ's message. Love of neighbor never suffers from unemployment or short hours. We do not need to say very much about it here: two simple quotations from the words of our Lord are more than enough: "I give you a new commandment: Love one another. Such as my love has been for you, so must your love be for each other. This is how all will know you for my disciples" (Jn 13:34-35). "Treat others the way you would have them treat you: this sums up the law and the prophets" (Mt 7:12).

This, then, is how we should pray: Dear God, make the evil folk good and the good folk a bit nicer (proverb). Take away from us our hardness of heart; take away "our stony hearts" and give us natural hearts (Ezk 36:26).

7.8 "Serve one another in love" (Gal 5:13)

7.8.0　　In a woven fabric I can be one thread, one nuance of color. Deep blue? Brilliant red? Or just the grey background thread? This "third color," as weavers call it, is the most important of all. Only the neutral grey of everyday living can bring out the depth of the blue or the brilliance of the red. This grey thread provides the harmony. It is sufficient for me to have my own color and to be glad that it can produce joy and not rivalry, as if I, the blue, were an enemy of the green. And those who either cannot or will not work together in the weaving? Can I not perhaps anticipate them and make room for them, so that they can thread their own color into the weaving? There is room for all. And each color contributes to the work of the weaving. Every one, not just those that were stretched over the frame at the beginning of the work. If one of the threads tears out, then the whole work has to stop and the weaver's hands must busy themselves with putting the thread back into place again.

Every thread, even the most brilliant, can disappear and, woven in with all the others, come to an end. But it is still there and has not disappeared, even though my eye can no longer perceive it. Now it is my turn to work my own thread into the whole weaving that surrounds me. If its end is no longer recognizable, then the harmony of the whole takes over. The harmony of all the colors accompanies the coloring of my own thread, until it disappears.

I do not know what will become of the weaving. Will I ever see it done? Or will it ever reach a conclusion? Your countenance remains open, You, risen from the dead (A Finnish weaver).

7.8.1 Baptism: call to service. In the First Letter to the Corinthians (1 Cor 12:12-31), St. Paul says that every believer who has been baptized is a member of the Body of Christ. Each one has his own essential mission in and for the whole; each one is in his own way a servant of the community. The individual ministries and charisms are all oriented towards each other, and each one is unique and irreplaceable (Rm 12:3-8). The Church cannot do without either the consecrated official or the dedicated layman. That is why there must never be any conflict between the hierarchic and the charismatic; between the official Church and the Church of love.

7.8.2 Authority: service in unity. "When they had eaten their meal, Jesus said to Simon Peter, 'Simon, do you love me more than these?' 'Yes, Lord,' he said, 'you know that I love you.' At which Jesus said, 'Feed my lambs' " (Jn 21:15). Here we see the pastoral office of the Church expressly linked to friendship with Christ. Authority in the Church is first and foremost friendship with the Lord. It is for this reason that it is essentially a service for the brethren. It can never be a claim to power. Ordained officials especially must heed these words: "Comfort and upbuild one another. . . . Remain at peace with one another. We exhort you to admonish the unruly; cheer the fainthearted; support the weak; be patient toward all. . . . Do not stifle the Spirit" (1 Th 5:11, 13, 14, 19). "All those who enjoy a position of leadership must consider themselves as servants of their brothers" (John XXIII).

Authority builds up the Body of Christ, and is geared towards the proper ordering of the various ministries. Roger Schutz has described this concept in brilliant terms: Authority in the Church has the mission to effect unity. It is there in order to gather and lead back together, over and over again, whatever tends to disassociate itself and form an opposition. The man who has the office of authority is first of all a servant. If he knows this, he will guard against the temptation of behaving in a paternalistic way. His service consists in directing the community in such a way that unity of will and spirit is its constant attitude; so that all its members are of one heart and soul and mind. This service for unity places the man who performs it, not at the peak of a pyramid, but in the middle of a community.

7.8.3 Religious Orders: living in the midst. The Church synod of the Federal Republic of Germany introduces its conclusions about religious orders in these words:

Spiritual communities were often God's call to their times. In their first beginnings, and wherever the spirit of their origins has remained alive, they have emanated a lasting impulse. They were cells of Christian renewal, communities of prayer. They addressed themselves to new objectives that were vital for the mission of the Church, and set out to counter the crises of their epochs. Our present unrest calls for similar help. From our spiritual communities we look for orientation in the question of the meaning of life, encouragement in faith, dedication to prayer and meditation, and a testimony of brotherly communal life and openness towards our fellow man. Their attitudes toward personal property, human sexuality, achievement, standards of living and careers should be of significance for every set of values that corresponds to the Gospel.

The people of God today do not need religious functionaries, pious pessimists, or anxious problem makers. The greatest blessing that the monastic communities could confer upon their brothers and sisters in the faith is simply this: to be truly believing persons who are living in our midst, people who live the demands of the Gospel radically and seriously, and who constantly grow in their fidelity to the Gospel ideals. They should be people who go along their way with joy and trust and radiant confidence, who live their decision for Christ without regret, and who serve as pioneers in the pilgrimage of God's people on earth.

7.8.4 Religious Orders: symbols of the imitation of Christ. Lay people expect a lot from religious. In one of the Swiss synods in 1972, a married woman put it like this:

> We lay people, who are trying to live according to the Gospel in the uproar and turmoil of our time, look upon the religious communities as visible signs of the imitation of Christ. They live an example of poverty for us in a society which has fallen prey to materialism. For centuries they have been examples for social work, and have cooperated in a decisive way in establishing the cultural values of our western culture. By their celibacy they are free to work undividedly for the Lord, and do what is pleasing to God, as St. Paul says in his First Letter to the Corinthians.
>
> At the same time, we interpret their life as a service of prayer for all mankind and for the world, whether it be a prayer of adoration or of petition. It is through the religious communities that we can most clearly see the claims God makes upon mankind.

We lay people, however, do not only need the religious communities as visible signs of the imitation of Christ; we turn to many of them in the hope that they will open their doors to us, and give us the opportunity to share in their prayer and meditation. In their houses we look for quiet, calm, and peace, so that we can draw new strength for our manifold duties in life, and fulfill them in the spirit of the Gospel.

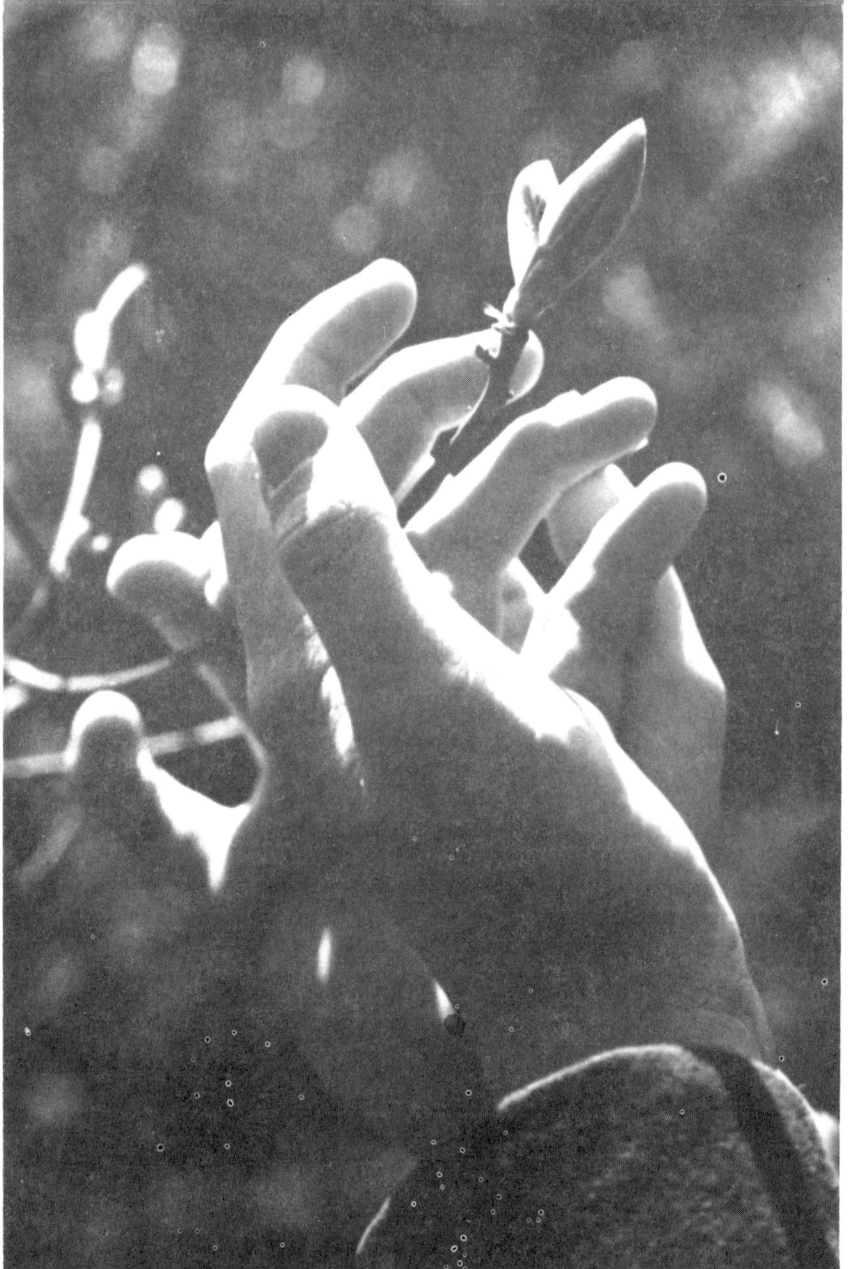

PART THREE:

CHRISTIAN FAITH IS WORLD-ORIENTED

8. FAITH OPEN TO THE WORLD

8.0 The way of faith does not lead out of the world, but right into its midst. Does being a stranger to the world make us any more pious? It would be a very serious mistake for a Christian to maintain this. Flight from creation is equivalent to flight from God. As believers, we must never flee from the world; for the visible universe is the theatre not only of all human history, but of salvation history as well. Even the holiest Christian is still a citizen of this world.

8.1 The world: temptation or way to God?

Creation is God's revelation. The first sentence of Scripture, "In the beginning God created heaven and earth," is not only a confession of the Creator, but also a confession of his creation. And our Creed begins with similar words: "I believe in God, the Father Almighty, Creator of heaven and earth." This, too, is a confession of the Creator and his work.

The Incarnation of Christ is God's boldest gift to this world. He lays claim upon everything that belongs to man, to his body and all of visible creation. God is interested in the little piece of the world that we are building up. His interest will continue all throughout time, until he returns at the very end of the world.

This is the real reason why the world is not primarily a temptation for us: it is supposed to be a way to God. And no man on earth can love creation and our world so passionately as the Christian can. Here, too, it is true that faith is friendship, friendship for the whole world.

8.2 Infatuated with the world

8.2.0 Faith interprets the world from the point of view of God; from creation to creator and from creator to creation. Christian faith compels us to view the visible and the invisible together, the earthly and the divine.

How tenderly a man like Francis of Assisi loved creation. For him, all things were transparent with God; he felt himself linked in ties of brotherhood with all the world. In his famous Canticle of the Sun, he sings of sun and water as sisters, wind and fire as brothers, earth as a mother.

8.2.1 *Beloved world?* Modern man has an appetite for the earthly. He has developed a passionate attachment for the world of things. We love the earth; we cling to this world; we are a part of it and feel at home here. And that is as it should be. Even the Christian is not hurt by a little "worldliness" of this kind. But have we really kept faith with mother earth? Do we love the things of earth correctly or incorrectly; as Christians or as white-washed heathens?

8.2.2 *Nostalgia: for earth, our home.* Have we not grown too used to our good earth? Perhaps a space flight would be good for us, a healthy distance from earth, in order to rediscover it for ourselves.

"On the return flight, when I saw the earth suddenly appear as a small blue sphere, I was seized with a powerful love for it, and I resolved to do everything I could to help save it." Neil Armstrong, the first man to walk upon the moon, made this solemn pronouncement. A powerful love for earth, and a resolution to save it!

James Irwin, another astronaut, expresses his feelings like this: "The earth is fantastic and beautiful, the one warm and living object we saw on our flight through space."

And astronaut Jack Swingert: "The earth has never appeared so desirable as out there in the lifeless infinity of space." Homesickness is love!

8.3 God's gift to the world

8.3.0 When the astronauts in Apollo X orbited around the moon, deeply stirred and with emotion in their voices, they read the Biblical account of creation: "In the beginning God made heaven and earth. . . ." Millions of TV viewers and radio listeners heard this proclamation from "on high."

8.3.1 *"In the beginning God made . . ." (Gn 1:1).* Faith itself tells us that ours is a beloved world. Out of love, God created it. "For you love all things that are and loathe nothing that you have made; for what you hated, you would not have fashioned. . . . You spare all things, because they are yours, O Lord and lover of souls" (Ws 11:24, 26).

The Creator was, ultimately, concerned with man. It is for man's sake that he loves the world. After God had called everything into existence out of nothingness, he made the king of creation from the dust of the earth. Man, in his body, is related to the earth. Then God immediately escorted man into the world of paradise, which was destined to serve as his dwelling place (Gn 2:8), and provide him with nourishment.

8.3.2 "God so loved the world . . ." (Jn 3:16). Powerful love for the world—resolution to save it. Surely this concept cannot help but remind us of God's own visitation upon earth, his union with his creature man. "God so loved the world that he gave his only Son, that whoever believes in him may not die but may have eternal life" (Jn 3:16). God walked the path of incarnation; and thus to a certain degree he became part of this world. In the person of Jesus, God has visited this tiny blue sphere. And now, for us Christians, this insignificantly small planet has become the focus of the entire universe. Through the Incarnation of God, everything on earth has experienced an undreamed-of re-evaluation. God is oriented towards the world, and the world towards God.

8.4 Church for the world

8.4.0 "Never before in her history has the Church so deeply recognized the need to know the world in which she lives, to draw closer to the world, to understand it, to serve it and to proclaim the Gospel to it, and at the same time to go out to meet it in its rapid and continuous transformation" (Paul VI at the conclusion of the Second Vatican Council, Dec. 8, 1965).

8.4.1 The "hostile" sisters? In the last hundred years, the official position of the Church toward the world has fundamentally altered. These two "hostile" sisters have come closer and closer together: the mistrust and suspicion of the mid-nineteenth century have yielded to the progressive dialogue of our modern times.

In broad (perhaps unforgivably so) outlines, we might sketch the relationship of Church and world as follows: Church against the world (Pius IX: 1846-1878); Church with the world (Leo XIII, Pius X, Benedict XV: 1878-1922); Church in the world (Pius XI, Pius XII: 1922-1958); Church for the world (John XXIII, Paul VI, John Paul I, John Paul II: since 1958).

8.4.2 Dialogue and service. This radical change in attitude is very clearly expressed in countless texts from the Second Vatican Council and from the pronouncements of recent pontiffs. The Church is entering into a dialogue with the world, in order to serve the world. The Church can no longer be content simply to contemplate its own navel. The Church has to continue the work of the Incarnation. It has to become more and more the Church for all the world.

> We dare not forget the optimism as well, or, to put it more properly, the love with which the Church of the Council looks upon the world in which she too finds herself. The Christian's eye remains fixed upon our moden world too. But the Christian does not fear the world, and does not withdraw from it; rather he looks upon it and blesses it. He looks upon it and blesses all the activities of mankind, science, labor, society. He sees, as always, the grandeur and the misery. But today, primarily, there is something more: the Church sees her call, her mission, the need of her presence. . . . You must understand that from now on we must educate ourselves to this conception of the Church and the world (Paul VI).

8.5 Steward and shaper of creation

8.5.0 Man is the beneficiary of his world and everything in it. There is no great need to dwell on this subject. It was for the sake of man that God created everything. And he entrusted everything to him: plants, trees, animals, all were meant to serve him (Gn 1:26, 28-29).

8.5.1 God's partner. God has great trust in man. He creates him in his own image, endows him with freedom, and gives him a share in the divine creative activity. God is neither a spoilsport nor an autocrat who thinks he has to do everything all by himself. He embarks upon an unheard-of risk: he entrusts creation itself to his most cherished creature. Man is to be his partner. God makes tremendous demands upon him, and takes him for his co-worker.

Man, for his part, knows more about his likeness to God than he ever has before (technology, medical progress, etc.). But does he have any better appreciation of who it is that wants him to be so "like unto God" (Ps 8:6)? Does he have any better appreciation of how his creator has entrusted him with personal freedom and responsibility?

8.5.2 Steward. It is, of course, true that God remains the real and ultimate proprietor of creation. But man is privileged to be his representative, and the steward of all the earth. The Bible depicts this truth in a bold figure: "Then the Lord God planted a garden in Eden, in the east, and he placed there the man whom he had formed . . . to cultivate it and to care for it" (Gn 2: 8, 15). Co-worker of God!

8.5.3 Shaper. "Fill the earth and subdue it" (Gn 1:28). What God is saying to man is this: "I have placed magnificent powers in the world of nature. It is your task to discover them in wonder, to evaluate them and harness them. I entrust you with the bare framework and the raw materials. It is up to you to make the world more livable and more human. The world is supposed to be your work, too."

And indeed, we encounter everywhere upon earth the traces of man's activity. Streets and cities, machines and satellites—he has made them all. Man is constantly at work, cooperating in the development of the world. Man has become the architect. And today he sees the world, not so much as an object of contemplation and wonder, but as material for his further activity.

8.5.4 Lord. Man, however, is in a position to be much more than merely the steward and shaper of creation. He is its lord. "Fill the earth and subdue it." "You have given him rule over the works of your hands, putting all things under his feet" (Ps 8:7).

This dominion over the world endows man with a truly unlimited power. He has become the great world engineer, almost a second creator. Unfortunately, in the process he often loses sight of the first Creator.

We Christians must see human work, progress and technology in this perspective. And we must never overlook the fact that being lord means being servant.

8.6 The purpose of work

8.6.0 Through history, work has been either praised to the skies or condemned to hell. It has been seen sometimes as the doing of the devil, and sometimes as a sharing with God himself. It has been described as both a blessing and a curse. There have been those who claim that man lives only to work, and those who claim that human work is like any other merchandise, something that a man is supposed to sell for a just price, his wages.

Truly we do not have any grounds for an exaggerated glorification of work. Work is also a burden and a pain. But the Christian has to ask himself, in the light of his faith: what is the purpose of work?

8.6.1 Work: gain. It is obvious that we work in order to earn. Nobody could deny that, or try to change it. But is that all that work really is? How much is earned by the mother who changes her infant child, or who stays up all night sitting by his sickbed? How much does she get for a bonus, for dirty work or for overtime? Work is for gain, indeed; but primarily and ultimately it is service: service to God and to our brother.

8.6.2 Work: service to God. We are privileged, and obligated, to be God's co-workers. And thus, we don't need to feel guilty if we make a truly responsible effort to change the world. There is no need for a bad conscience. The Bible itself encourages man to make progress in science and technology. "Fill the earth and subdue it." God has placed unheard-of powers and energies into the world. But he did not build any steam engines, or autos, or space ships. The Christian realizes that he is able to, and expected to, cooperate in the completion of creation. In this work, he is not alone. The Creator God is present, from the very beginning, in the workshop and on the building site. Work, properly understood, means service to God. Service to the world—service to God. In this sense, we can say that work is also prayer.

8.6.3 Work: service to mankind. In his work, man expresses his own self. At the same time he can, through his work, make a contribution towards a better world. Work is not only an act that shares in creation; it is even more a service to the human community. God makes available to us many of the good things of this world in an unfinished form. It is the work of our hands that prepares them for our use. The wheat does indeed grow in the field, but not the bread. God provides us with our daily bread only through the hands of the baker. How many men had to work and invent before we were able to have a single piece of bread on the table! Then there are carpenters and cabinet makers and plumbers and electricians, to build our houses for us. This is how they serve us. Work is service to mankind.

There is a great variety of talents, capacities, and vocations. And all of them mutually complement each other. Not all men can be senators and congressmen. In our society there also have to be housewives and doctors, waiters and priests, cooks and politicians, factory workers and teachers. We are all oriented towards each other. Work unites mankind;

it is a form of service to our brothers and sisters, a way of loving our neighbor.

In the Eucharist, Christ shows us how seriously he takes our work. Bread consists of several thousand grains of wheat. In the Eucharist, bread, the fruit of our earth and of our work, becomes the body of Christ. It is a symbol of unity with the Lord and with our brothers.

8.7 Progress and technology

8.7.0 Modern man works furiously to continue the activity of creation. And his gigantic efforts have accomplished truly amazing results. His creative passion leads him into the boldest adventures. In contemplating his scientific and technological accomplishments, he is frequently overcome by an intoxication of awe. Modern man is dominated by a strong awareness of his own power. He knows that he is called to progress; and he also knows that he is in possession of the necessary means.

8.7.1 A second Creator? Our scientific and technological progress, in this century, has accelerated at a dizzying pace. Ours has been called the age of the atom, the age of mastery of space, the age of artificial materialism, of the mass media, of cybernetics, and of electronics.

On July 16, 1945, with the explosion of the first atom bomb, the atomic age began. On October 4, 1957, the Russian Sputnik I became the first artificial satellite to circle the globe. On July 20, 1969, man first set foot on the moon. When Neil Armstrong leaped down from his space ship, he said: "That's one small step for a man, one giant leap for mankind." Science and technology make it possible for man to reach for the stars, for the universe. He is becoming more and more the master of a reality that he is rationally planning, shaping, and directing. Will this make him a rival to God?

8.7.2 Rivals of the Creator? The Christian sees technology not as the work of the devil, but rather as a form of "filling and subduing the earth" in the sense of the Creator's mandate. God has entrusted mankind with his creation, including all of its marvelous powers. He did not shrink from entering upon this risk.

We must not, however, fall prey to a naive credulity in human progress. Technology makes it possible for us to draw nearer to God and to our fellow man, but also nearer to a world of demons. Obviously, a non-Christian can be just as responsible and effective with technology as a Christian. But still, Christian faith does have something to do with technology and progress. Things can become truly dangerous when a soulless technology wins control over humanity, or when an arrogant humanity dissolves its bonds with God and tries to be his competitor rather than his partner.

If the second creator loses his awareness of responsibility, then he is no longer in a position to have dominion over the world and over his own accomplishments. Then man will be threatened by his own works. Today, therefore, it is within man's power to annihilate himself and the world he lives in. But, on the other hand, the deeper mankind penetrates into the mystery of the universe—its laws and rhythm and functioning—the more will he have to admit in wonder and humility: "How modest are our works in comparison with your work, O God!"

8.8 Christian responsibility for the world

8.8.0 God has endowed man, the lord and steward of this earth, with freedom. But being free means taking on some responsibility. Man has to take responsibility for what becomes of the world.

8.8.1 Misuse of power. Scientists and politicians paint a gloomy picture of our environment. Gasses and chemical vapors contaminate our air.

Traffic noises and the stench of gasoline fumes threaten mankind. Many of our ponds are polluted with oil and infected with bacteria. Many of our lakes have turned into fish-destroying sewers. Rivers have been enslaved to serve as sources of energy. There is wide-scale violence to nature, and great destruction of our landscape. Climatic changes and new kinds of diseases have made their appearance.

It is obvious that we have done something wrong, and have tampered with some balances of life and nature vital to our survival. Irreplaceable sources of energy appear to be running out. Worldwide supplies of vital raw materials are disappearing. We are disfiguring nature and the beautiful face of the earth. Over-exploitation of resources and other sins against ecology are the order of the day.

Suddenly, we begin to get worried. We are faced with a problem of survival: will it still be possible tomorrow for men and animals to live? Has our control over the world gone astray? Can man dare to interfere so blindly in the world of nature, and continue to ravage and plunder our mother the earth so thoughtlessly?

All these reflections must indeed open our eyes to the real concerns of our modern world. We must realize that we cannot simply go on in this way. We must rethink our position, and retrace our steps.

8.8.2 Rethinking. Science and technology have immeasurably increased human responsibility. The technological achievements we enjoy can also be misused for evil purposes. Technological progress, once set free from the proper exercise of human responsibility, can only lead to tragedy.

We are faced with the question of whether man, who today can accomplish practically anything he wills, is also justified in wanting the things he is able to accomplish.

We must convert; that is, we must rethink. Conversion to God involves, today more than ever, a conversion to the world as well. We cannot merely do what we will with our world. It does not belong to our generation alone. It is a world for the generations to come, and it must provide room for all to live. What kind of world will we leave to the people of tomorrow? Conversion, in this context, means observing solidarity with future generations, too, and recognizing our responsibility to them. We must share with them. We are tenants upon this earth, and our ancestors were fellow-tenants, as will be our descendants. We do not inherit the world from our fathers; no, we lease it from our children.

8.8.3 Making sacrifices. It cannot go on this way! A little reflection is enough to convince us. We must fundamentally change our basic position. The Christian way of life has always involved making sacrifices. Today, it demands that we engage in a battle against profligate waste, that we conserve energy, cut down our consumption, and adopt a simpler style of life. Responsibility for the world means planning and economizing, doing without and saving. We have to live differently, for other people to live at all.

8.8.4 Ecology. Creation is more than the sum of its individual elements. All things embrace one another. The relationship between us and them should be one of friendship. Ecology is a new virtue for the man of today. Not only man, but all the universe is the creation of God. Must we not learn to have a more profound reverence for creation? When we lose respect for nature, we also lose respect for mankind. Only when we have a reverence for the universe as a whole (people and animals, plants and all of nature), can we respect the works of God.

It would be a terrible shame if we learn only through our catastrophes. Today, it is the mission of the Church to cooperate in the formation of this awareness. Together with all people of good will, the Christian must assume responsibility for the common future of mankind and the whole world. Man's true service consists in a loving relationship with nature, acting as a careful guardian. Concern for ecology is, in the last analysis, concern for the preservation of mankind. What is at stake here is a world to live in.

8.9 "Justice and peace shall kiss" (Ps 85:11)

8.9.0 A Christianity that preaches only the hereafter, and avoids having anything to do with political and social issues, is overlooking an essential part of its mandate. Christian faith has something to do with politics. Politics involves an assumption of responsibility for the community, for the common good, and for society and the world. Concern for peace and social justice is also a way of exercising the love of neighbor commanded by Christ. That is why peace and justice are inseparable. "Peace is not simply non-war. It is in a true and proper sense the work of justice" (Second Vatican Council). And thus, the teaching office of the Church must take positions on political and social questions, too.

8.9.1 Shalom! Shalom! It is not an easy matter to translate this Hebrew word into English. *Shalom* implies the well-being of both the individual and the community. It also conveys the idea of the proper relationship between individuals and nations. Jesus Christ is our *shalom*, our peace (Ep 2:14). On the cross, he established peace (Col 1:20). St. Paul has left us this moving description of what *shalom* must mean for us Christians: "Over all these virtues put on love, which binds the rest together and makes them perfect" (Col 3:14). *Shalom* thus means: blessing, liberation, reconciliation, peace, harmony, brotherly love, security in society, friendship, all-embracing salvation—in a word, redemption and the heart of the Gospel. That is why the effort to establish *shalom*, peace in the world, is one of the fundamental demands of our faith. This basic demand of the Gospel extends to the problems of war and conscientious objection, the arms race and the weapons trade, terror and non-violence.

8.9.2 "Right and justice upon earth" (Jr 23:5). Lasting peace is based upon justice. During their General Chapter in 1979, the Redemptorists assembled in Rome made several pronouncements on the subject of social justice and evangelization. Here is the gist of some of their deliberations.

In our world live countless people who are the victims of injustice. Frequently we no longer hear their cry. They no longer have any voice, because they have violently been forced into silence. If we think back upon the innermost core of Jesus' message, we must clearly recognize the fact that our God is on the side of the poor. He takes a stand for the oppressed and for those whose lives fall short of their expectations. The Gospel of Jesus Christ is aimed at the redemption and liberation of the whole person. Christian faith, preaching the Gospel, love of neighbor, concern for justice—these are all inseparable.

As Christians and as religious, we must therefore try to live justice ourselves, among each other; unite ourselves with the fate of the poor; and take a stand on behalf of the rights of man and his complete liberation.

In this work, we must make every conceivable effort to avoid any trace of paternalism, conscious or even unconscious presumption, and any attempt to act as chaperons. We must help the oppressed to overcome the things that condemn them to live on the outer edges of life (hunger, illiteracy, injustice and oppression in every form).

The poor, for their part, often possess values which we have largely lost sight of. If we listen closely, they, for their part, can provide us with many gifts and make a great contribution to our conversion. We will be both givers and receivers. Only if both parties take the partnership seriously, will their liberation succeed in avoiding a new enslavement or dependency. Faith is friendship and solidarity with the poor.

8.9.3 Human rights. On December 10, 1948, the General Assembly of the United Nations approved and proclaimed the General Declaration of Human Rights. On closer examination, we can see that this document incorporates a fundamental concern of the preaching of Christ: the dignity, freedom, development and respect of every human person, everywhere and always. Fundamentally, all people are of equal worth, and thus each one deserves the same fundamental dignity and rights. Here the Gospel becomes concrete and obligatory for our daily activity, both in our little world and in the greater world of human experience.

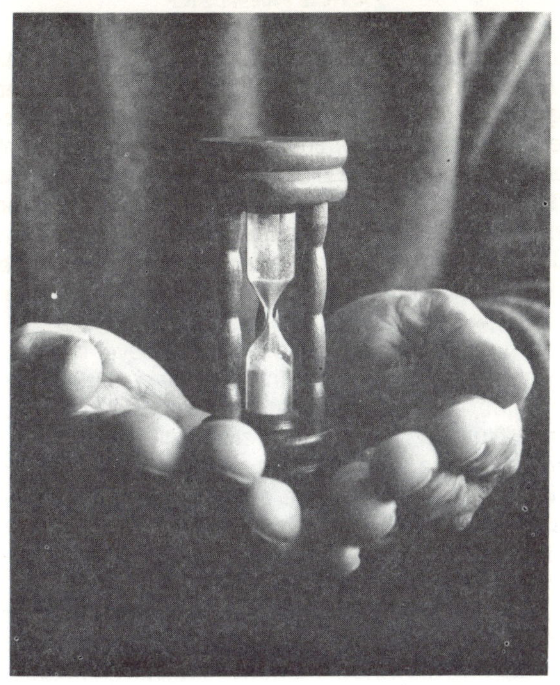

PART FOUR:

CHRISTIAN FAITH IS HISTORY-ORIENTED

9. HISTORICAL FAITH

9.0 The mystery of time

From time immemorial, we have puzzled over the mystery of time. Man, your life is ticking away. No matter what is happening in your life, the clock is always setting the tempo. The clock strikes at the coffins of friends and parents; it strikes above my cradle, and it will strike when my heart has stilled.

A philosopher in the Old Testament has this to say: "There is an appointed time for everything, and a time for every affair under the heavens. A time to be born and a time to die. . . . A time to weep, and a time to laugh. . . . A time to be silent and a time to speak" (Ec 3:1, 2, 4, 7).

9.0.0 Time is precious. Time can be precious. In sports, in the Olympic Games, we are well aware of this fact. How tense and concentrated is the skier, the sprinter. Only one thing matters: to get to the finish line as quickly and safely as possible. The deciding margin may be measured in hundredths of a second. The Bible encourages us to take an example from the athletes, and, like them, to treasure the moment and to make good use of time (Ep 5:16). "My entire attention is on the finish line as I run toward the prize to which God calls me—life on high in Christ Jesus" (Ph 3:14).

9.0.1 Time: a fugitive present. Who of us has never been frightened by the mystery of time? During our earthly pilgrimage, we live and encounter each other in time. We cannot escape it. But it can easily slip away from us. It runs; it flies. In this age of hectic activity, we run around like chickens with their heads cut off. And always, "we have no time."

Time is a fugitive present. We receive it drop by drop. If it came in one lump sum, wholesale, we could never bear up under the total burden of the combined time of our whole life. If we could know everything that the future would bring, we could never bear the burden.

We always live only in the one single moment of the present, the here and now. What was, we assimilate in the present now, into the future still to come. This is how it is with breathing, and with the beating of the heart. This is how it is everywhere in our human life.

9.0.2 Time: gift for friendship. We measure time with hour-glasses and water-clocks, with sundials and mechanical clocks and quartz watches. We count in terms of lunar and solar years. But our measurement of time does not always coincide with our experience of it. For people in love, time seems to stand still. For sick people, it can be stubbornly slow and as monotonous as death itself. One and the same hour can be hardly perceptible for the happy person, while for the dying man it can stretch on "without end."

One more thing. The serious and the tragic are an essential part of time. Time is the framework in which a man's decisive steps are taken. It is in temporal events that the consummation begins; the true meaning of time is "friendship." In the framework of time we can make the things of the world, our fellow mortals, and even God objects of intimacy. Friends can "wait" for each other: time is a gift of friendship. That was the mystery of the Little Prince: "It is the time you have wasted for your rose that makes your rose so important."

9.1 History: sister of time

9.1.0 History! This is the name we give to the great relative, the sister of time. Man, like no other creature, is oriented to history. This is not only because his life is embedded into the history of all humanity and creation. This is not only because he is constantly on the way between past and future, between being and becoming. Wherever there is a question of history, there is man at work; there he is involved. He is the chief actor of history, and history is largely determined by human freedom.

9.1.1 History means being on the way. History is much more than an orderly series of historical dates and events. What is essential to the concept of history is flux, what we call change and motion. On the way! The universe is moving fast. The Cancer nebula, the remnant of a stellar explosion, is bursting apart from its center even today at a speed of more than 1776 miles every second.

Never before has man had such a finely-tuned sense for evolution and development, transformation and history. Something new is always coming to light. Living habits and mass communications, dress and fashion, buildings and styles of residence, our feeling for life and our ways of thinking—all these things have been fundamentally changed in the span of a single human life. We can easily see that man, like the rest of creation, is "on the way."

9.1.2 History means remembering. History lives upon the past. History would be unthinkable without community and tradition, without language and symbol. It is the remembrance of love and joy that were given and received earlier; of blood and tears that have already flowed. It is the story of those from whom we have our life. Tradition, into the living present!

9.1.3 History means hope. Just as history is involved with remembrance of the past, so is it bound up with hope in what is promised. Man lives on hope. Lovers hope for a happy future because they have experienced happiness together in the past. For them, there is no trusting in time. And thus, even the remembrance of past good deeds can be a spur towards the future. The trust which is born of experience flows into the present, giving it direction and helping to bring the future into being.

9.2 God's history with man

9.2.0 "In times past, God spoke in fragmentary and varied ways to our fathers through the prophets; in this, the final age, he has spoken to us through his Son, whom he has made heir of all things and through whom he first created the universe. . . . He sustains all things by his powerful word. When he had cleansed us from our sins, he took his seat at the right hand of the Majesty in heaven" (Heb 1:1-3).

9.2.1 Salvation History. Faith is friendship. Like every other friendship, it is related to history. God is neither silent, nor hidden. He makes his way into human history. He seeks man out and acts in the world of time, to save man and his world. Since God reveals himself in history, we can speak about the history of revelation, salvation history. By this, we mean the historical dialogue between God and man: a series of divine initiatives and human responses. Salvation history is the living encounter between God and man. It encompasses God's approach to man, and man's acceptance or rejection of these overtures.

9.2.2 God on the way. The Bible describes salvation history for us. This history is one of life, transformation, unrest and activity. Yes, in the Bible, too, there is activity and movement. The sacred text proclaims a God who accompanies man on his walk through history. In the Old Testament alone, the name "Yahweh" occurs more than 6800 times. The unnamed God has revealed his name: "I am here and I will be here: with you and for you."

God creates the world and mankind. He is the God of Abraham, Isaac, and Jacob; the God of history; the God who freed his people and led them out of Egypt. For the Israelite, the focus of faith was the Passover, the festival of liberation. "It is the Passover of the Lord" (Ex 12:11). The Lord himself passed by, to redeem his people. God has revealed himself through definite and decisive events in history (Ps 78). "Think back on the days of old, reflect on the years of age upon age. Ask your father and he will inform you, ask your elders and they will tell you" (Dt 32:7).

God has made history with us, not by giving us things, but by giving himself. This "God with us" revealed himself in the person of Jesus Christ, whose name is Emmanuel, that is, "God with us." In Jesus, too, everything is history and event. This is how the four Evangelists report the life of Jesus; his words and his acts; his death and resurrection. In Jesus, God is on the way. His life is a pilgrimage. Mary carries him in her womb. She hastens into the mountain country, to carry him to Elizabeth (Lk 1:39-56). She carries him to Bethlehem, so that he can be born there (Lk 2:1-7). He has to flee into Egypt (Mt 2:13-15); he makes a pilgrimage to Jerusalem (Lk 2:41-50); in the role of traveling preacher he makes his way from one region to another; he goes along his way of the cross (Lk 23:26-33).

Even the earliest Christian creeds are a confession of God's historical activity in the person of Jesus Christ. One of the most important of these formulas of faith is to be found in the First Letter to the Corinthians: "Christ died for our sins in accordance with the Scriptures; he was buried and, in accordance with the Scriptures, rose on the third day. He was seen by Cephas, then by the Twelve. After that he was seen by five hundred brothers at once. . . ." (1 Cor 15:3-6). Two thousand years later, Christ is not simply a memory: he is alive and at work today.

9.2.3 God calls us to activity. God, then, is himself "on the way," at work in the world. But this God of the universe also acts as our leader. When God comes, he sets mankind into activity. He makes them restless, and sends them out on pilgrimage. He is their leader. Abraham leaves his home and country: "Go out of your land" (Gn 12:1). Moses, with all his people, makes his way through the wilderness to the Promised Land. God sends this pilgrim people on its way and makes them active, in order to give them the gift of redemption. For the Jews, the festival of Passover is the celebration of their release from the slavery of Egypt: it is a celebration of setting out and starting a journey.

The Virgin Mary, too, is on her way (Mt 2:14; Lk 1:39, 2:4-5). The shepherds, for their part, are in a hurry to seek out the Christ Child (Lk 2:15-16). From the Orient, the Magi set out on their way to find Jesus (Mt 2:1-2). The Apostles travel from one country to another.

The Christian is, in his faith, always on the way. Israel's faith was bound up with history, and was characterized by a good deal of restlessness. Being a Christian means being on one's way in faith.

9.2.4 God is faithful. Fidelity is love that lasts. In the change and confusion of history, there is one thing that remains constant: God's fidelity. The continuing story of God's activity with mankind is salvation history only because, in the ebb and flow of human history, the love of God remains unswervingly constant. "God is faithful" (1 Cor 1:9). Heaven has a good memory!

God is faithful. It is in Christ that he has given a definitive proof of his fidelity. "Whatever promises God has made have been fulfilled in Christ" (2 Cor 1:20). In Christ he has fulfilled all things (Lk 24:25-27, 44-45). And "Christ remains the same yesterday, today, and for all eternity" (Heb 13:8). He *is* fidelity (2 Tm 2:13). "Whatever promises God has made have been fulfilled in him; therefore it is through him that we address our

Amen to God when we worship together. God is the one who firmly establishes us along with you in Christ" (2 Cor 1:20-21).

That is why the believer must not assume an air of catastrophe. He must repond, instead, with quiet hope in the face of all the disturbing events that characterize our age of upheaval. He must always answer: "The man who has faith does not need to tremble." The faithful Christian need not experience anxiety in the face of history. He remembers the promises of God. He recalls how many of our brothers, in times past, have had experiences of God's fidelity; "for his faithfulness endures forever" (Ps 100:5).

9.2.5 Recollection and hope. Because God is faithful, Christian faith is a mixture of recollection and promise. In the field of tension generated by these two poles, we must establish our hope. Salvation history, as it is portrayed in the Bible, is a grand story of promise, a story of friendship. Whenever a promise is fulfilled, future hopes vie with each other in scope and intensity. The horizons of expectation continue to enlarge. Christian faith means being on the move with the impetus of a powerful hope.

The Second Vatican Council uses these words to describe the objective and panorama of salvation history:

> The Lord is the goal of all human history, the point towards which all the strivings and activities of history and culture converge, the focus of humanity, the joy of every heart and the fulfillment of every desire. Animated and united by his spirit, we make our way towards the fulfillment of human history, which coincides with the plan of his love, "to bring all things in the heavens and on earth into one under Christ's headship."

Christian faith, of course, is a virtue of dynamic action, not of passive submission. Before us, others have worked and wept and suffered. Many of them, in their faith, have enjoyed an experience of God. This must give us courage to continue towards the fulfillment of God's mighty promises. We have confidence that history—our own and that of all mankind—is progressing towards a happy ending. But this confidence must not lead us to a cowardly and premature flight into the hereafter. Ours must be a hope in the present, and a concern with the here and now. *Shalom* here below for today!

> See what love the Father has bestowed on us in letting us be called children of God! Yet that is what we are. . . . What we shall later be

has not yet come to light. We know that when it comes to light we shall be like him, for we shall see him as he is. Everyone who has this hope based on him keeps himself pure, as he is pure (1 Jn 3:1-3).

9.3 Underway in faith

9.3.0 "This is the time of fulfillment. The reign of God is at hand. Reform your lives and believe in the gospel" (Mk 1:15). The whole Bible describes this eagerness to press on ahead—from promise to fulfillment, and from one fulfillment to new promises. How much would be changed in our Church if we would allow our faith and prayer to enter solidly into the progression of history, and if we could understand it all from God's perspective!

9.3.1 The "Great Day." The end-time has already dawned. But the fulfillment and manifest revelation of the greatest of God's promises is yet to take place. "Men will see the Son of Man coming on a cloud with great power and glory. When these things begin to happen, stand erect and hold your heads high, for your deliverance is near at hand" (Lk 21:27-28).

The Lord will come again! No other event in the New Testament is stressed with such great urgency. Christ himself speaks of his coming in power and glory (Mt 26:64). He speaks of "his day" (Jn 8:56), of the "last day" (Jn 6:39).

St. Paul, for his part, depicts this great day in every conceivable tone and variation. He calls it the "day of the Lord" (1 Cor 1:8), the "day of salvation" (2 Cor 6:2), the "day of redemption" (Ep 4:30), the "day of the revelation of his glory" (2 Th 1:7).

The day of Christ's second coming is simply "the great day" (Jude 6). This day, with its indescribable promises, nourishes the hope of the Church and of the individual Christian (Ph 3:20-21). "Stand erect and hold your heads high, for your deliverance is near at hand" (Lk 21:28).

9.3.2 Already—not yet. It is in this tension between "already" and "not yet" that we Christians live. "In hope we were saved" (Rm 8:24). That is why we persevere and wait for the "revelation of our Lord Jesus Christ" (1 Cor 1:7). "We have our citizenship in heaven; it is from there that we eagerly await the coming of our Savior, the Lord Jesus Christ" (Ph 3:20). That is why ours is a "blessed hope" (Tt 2:13).

From this, we can readily see why faith is friendship from yet another point of view. The Hebrew word *Amen* (= believe) means, first of all, that something is fast and true, reliable and that it is true to its promise. God is fidelity. Believing means saying "Amen" to God; remaining bound to him in fidelity; committing oneself wholly to the reliability of God, and trusting implicitly in his promise. "Unless your faith is firm, you shall not be firm" (Is 7:9).

9.3.3 The time of faith. Faithfulness that lasts: this is friendship. Faithfulness that lasts: this is salvation history. Faithfulness that lasts: this is our faith. Faith is, accordingly, faithfulness that extends over time. It is a state of being "on the way." Faith is not something that "is," but rather something that keeps happening. We are never wholly in possession of faith; we are always in search of it. Throughout our life, we can never wholly grasp God and Christ. Augustine, that subtle thinker and great believer, expresses it in these words:

> Seek for God. We must seek for him in order to find him. We must seek for him after we have found him. In order for us to seek for him before we have found him, he is hidden. And in order for us to seek for him after we have found him, he is immeasurable, infinite. He can satisfy the man who seeks for him, insofar as the seeker can grasp him. And he makes the man who finds him capable of seeking for him further, seeking to be filled.

Never do we believe enough, just as people in love can never really love each other enough. Faith is a lifelong task, and always requires fresh effort. It can grow and mature; it can wither and die.

9.3.4 "Lived" faith. Faith is like warmth: it shares itself. We take it in from our mother, together with the warmth of her breast, with her milk, from her lips. That is when we begin to have faith; just as we stop freezing as soon as we touch something warm. For me, faith is first of all my mother's warmth: life itself. It is something given to us immediately together with life itself, by our mother (Virgil Gheorghiu).

Today, it is difficult to share views like these. Is there really such a simple and direct "lived" faith in our de-Christianized world of today? Is it not true that faith is much more dependent upon our personal decision and conviction? No matter what the case may be, the influence of our parents is just as essential an element today as it has ever been. Our mother, especially, is and remains the very first teacher to shape the elements of faith in the child. It is she who lays the first foundations for the later experience of faith, and who initiates the child into the art of believing.

9.3.5 Faith is never at a standstill. Faith means encountering Christ, joining him along the way. For as long as the baptized believer lives, he can still lose his way; he can grow weary or simply lie down and give up. But he can also stride forward in his faith, and reach his goal.

Faith is like a stream of life, organic and dynamic. It has its birth and its death, its flood and its ebb, its forward steps and its backward steps. Faith is progress or it is decline, but it is never static. It never reaches its goal without passing over into vision.

It is because faith occurs in the context of history that it can always grow or decline, that it can always be won or lost or won again. The New Testament speaks of having faith and of growing in faith (1 Th 1:5-8), increase in faith (2 Th 1:3), development of faith (Lk 17:5-6), being strong or being weak in faith (Rm 4:19), standing fast in faith (Col 2:7), being constant in faith (Col 1:23), being steadfast in faith (1 P 5:9), being strong in faith (Ac 16:5), holding to faith (2 Tm 4:7), persevering in faith (Jm 1:3), abiding in faith (Heb 12:2, 28), persisting in faith (Ac 14:22), perfect faith (Heb 10:22-23), falsifying the faith (2 Tm 3:8), perverting the faith (Ac 20:30), losing the faith (1 Tm 4:1).

9.3.6 The age of faith. Faith, like human life, has various stages and ages. The child's faith is different from that of the adult, and different, too, from that of the old man.

A small child can easily attain a wonderfully genuine faith, but it remains the faith of a child. If a mature adult were to try to walk in a child's shoes, he would surely find them too small, and end up discarding them. Likewise, if a young man's faith grows no bigger than the faith of his childhood, it is static and useless. If he does not personally make his faith deeper and more profound, he will be smuggling an infantile faith into his later years. Soon, his life and his faith will no longer adequately match.

In every change-of-life situation, faith encounters a new experience: life and faith are intimately connected. During the years of courting, and in the course of married life, faith necessarily takes on a new form and configuration. Faith takes on a new tone; for man and woman mutually influence each other. For the older person, once again, the experience of faith is different. In a word, we are continually being called to conversion and decision. Faith is life: believing is living. Faith is always bound up with a situation; it has an historical orientation. Or, to put it in other words, each particular individual experience has its corresponding different experience of faith.

9.3.7 Stages of faith. Frequently, we evaluate people on the basis of their stages of faith. We speak of saints and atheists, of mystics and dissidents, of practicing and non-practicing Catholics, of marginal Christians, elite Christians, traditional Christians, churchless Christians, and non-Christians. Every rank and gradation is possible. Of course, any categorization that implies a judgment is out of place. All of us, especially priests, must be tolerant. God is at work in mankind, and long before the pastor begins his work. He, above all others, must strive to proceed at the same pace as God. The Holy Spirit does not overwhelm or destroy anything. The priest, in his pastoral ministry, must lead a man in the direction that God has already steered him. From that point onward, he must help him go even further.

9.3.8 Cultivation and deepening of faith. Faith is always a sort of hazard, and is never a guaranteed possession. It calls a man constantly forward, to a new confrontation and a new decision. Difficulties and doubts in faith are normal. My faith, too, will always be under attack, and must always be proved and tested.

Somehow, the believer always remains something of an unbeliever. Much in even the Christian heart remains unconverted. "I believe, Lord; help my unbelief" (Mk 9:24). That is why we must show great understanding for the crises in faith that many Christians experience. Crises in faith are, in fact, necessary in order to make our faith living and capable of resistance. It is these very crises that, for a man who honestly believes and searches, can serve as a purifying initiation into life with God.

Faith and "more faith" are not things we can simply buy at a self-service store. Often, we have to care for our faith with great pains, and cultivate and nourish it. We have to constantly work at deepening its roots and increasing its vitality: by listening to the word of God; by celebrating the Eucharist and the other sacraments; by prayer; by constant self-growth; by dedication to our day-to-day living.

9.4 Final destination: death?

9.4.0 "In the midst of life we are surrounded by death." Man always lives in the face of death. "You are dirt, and to dirt you shall return" (Gn 3:19).

In the very first pages of the Bible, we already encounter this tension between our will to live and the inevitability of death. Man carries within himself both an eager desire for life and an anxiety in the face of death. He wants to protect himself against death. That is why he is anxious. Anxiety like this is, in the final analysis, a protective function of human life.

Throughout our lives we experience death as spectators and observers. None of us has yet died. Moreover, modern people seldom have the opportunity to witness the actual death of another person. We almost never come into direct contact with death. Instead of relatives, machines now keep vigil at the deathbed. Death and dying surely still number among the most oppressively troublesome of all human questions. But these questions, and the answers to them, are today more likely to be suppressed than faced and overcome. One thing is certain: they cannot be ignored.

Each of us must die alone. No one can spare us. There can be no death by surrogate. And death will come "certain as death." The moment of death is the hour of truth: there is no more room for appearances or deception. Death is the dissolution of historical man, of human life as we record it in history. But then comes the question of whether there is anything left. What is the ultimate solution? Is death merely a descent into the grave? Is death the final destination—everybody out! What next?

9.4.1 Christ died for us. It might seem very strange to put it this way, but when the Christian asks about the problem of death, he is really asking about life. During his lifetime, Jesus encountered death several times (Lk 7:11-17, 8:41-56; Jn 11:1-44). He was disturbed at the sorrow of other people. He himself had little to say about death. But he took it seriously. Faced with the death of a friend, he wept (Jn 11:3-35). He himself suffered an agony at the prospect of death (Mk 14:34-36). His own death was not an easy one. After a loud cry of anguish, he bowed his head and died. But neither was his death a fiasco. Resurrection! That was, for him, the conquest of death. And since that time, in the eyes of faith, everything changed for us. "Death, where is your sting?" (1 Cor 15:55). And the Lord says: "I have the keys of death" (Rv 1:18). "I am the resurrection and the life; whoever believes in me, though he should die, will come to life; and whoever is alive and believes in me will never die" (Jn 11:25-26).

9.4.2 Do Christians die a different death? Even the Christian dies. Like everyone else, he finds death difficult. For him, too, it is the one great trial of his life. Even the most convinced faith does not resolve all the ques-

tions. And yet, this faith must completely change the death of the Christian.

Love denies death. "You must not die." This is the language of love. A person who is truly loved will know that even after his death, he is not dead for the one who loves him. "Love is stronger than death" (Sg 8:6). People in love cherish the confidence that even beyond the grave there is some place of future communion. Faith is friendship. Christian faith tells me that there is a love that will remain faithful to me beyond death. God will never take away my love, even at my death. I am saved in this love, and for this love. "With everlasting love I love you," says the Lord (Jr 31:3). In this love, I will never be dead. "I am certain that neither death nor life, neither height nor depth nor any other creature will be able to separate us from the love of God that comes to us in Christ Jesus, our Lord" (Rm 8:38-39).

As it was for Christ, so it is for each of the faithful. Death is no longer an end, but rather a transition. The man who believes commits himself into this merciful love of God. In death, God will come to meet us, like the kindly father in the parable of the Prodigal Son. He will not start by asking questions about guilt; he will draw us to himself in infinite love. And that—such is our hope—will be the true and proper experience of our Christian death. Thus, for us Christians death is, in the final analysis, a gift. This is providing that we love; for if a man does not love, he remains in death (1 Jn 3:14).

9.4.3 Day of death: day of friendship. We encounter God frequently during the course of our life. There can be encounters of genuine friendship with him. But in all these encounters, God remains hidden. He is silent. At death, however, we shall see him in a definitive way, face to face. St. Ignatius of Antioch (d. *circa* 110 A.D.) wrote the following to his fellow Christians who wanted to prevent his martyrdom: "Let me be. I want to go to the Lord. When I grasp his light, I will be a true man." St. Paul says the same thing: "I long to be freed from this life and to be with Christ" (Ph 1:23). This can only be the awareness of those who love and who believe in their friendship with God. Thus, for the man who believes, death is not an act of dying into nothingness, but an act of crossing over into resurrection. The overwhelming experience of faith means that we will die, but not be dead: "Both in life and death we are the Lord's" (Rm 14:8). We overcome the night of death by our hope. The day of death becomes the day of our return to God, a day of great friendship: our true and proper birthday, and the final fulfillment of our human person.

In death, we also meet God as members of a community of faith. Anytime a Christian dies anywhere in the world, a little bit of the Church has already arrived at its final destination.

The death of a person does not mark the end of their presence among the living. The Christian commemoration of the faithful departed is much more than a remembrance of loved ones who have passed away. The dead remain closely bound to us. We will see them once again, and be together with them in the Lord. Our prayers for the dead are a protest against forgetting them. "The man who lives in the hearts of his beloved is not dead; he is only distant. And the man who returns home to the Lord remains with his family" (Jerome). Our prayers for the deceased are also a confession of Christ's resurrection, which embraces both this world and the hereafter. Christ's resurrection unites us and the departed in the Communion of Saints.

9.4.4 We die many deaths. Dying is part of human dignity. Only man knows, his whole life long, that he is going to die. Our life is expressly oriented towards this death, and the decision it implies. But still God hides from us the precise moment of death, so that we will always be prepared, always waiting for it. That is why we are encouraged to vigilance: "The day of the Lord is coming like a thief in the night" (1 Th 5:2). The Christian must learn to die his death, not only in his final moments, but his whole life long. Our life is shot through with death. We are always having rehearsals. Man dies many deaths before he dies the last one (2 Cor 4:10). A good death is an art. Rilke speaks of a "well worked-out death." We must do everything we can to assure its success; for an unsuccessful death can never be repeated. From its very first moment, our life is already a form of dying. It takes on many different names: growing old, being sick, saying farewell.

9.4.5 Death: friend and brother. The closeness of death can give real depth to life. Lovers who have to say goodbye to each other are closer at that moment than they have ever been before. Death, to be sure, is an uninvited guest. But he will surely come. And thus, we should get to know and understand him.

Wolfgang Amadeus Mozart wrote a letter to his father when he was 32, just three years before his early death in 1787:

> "Dear Father! Since death is the ultimate purpose of our life, I have, during the past few years, made myself so acquainted with this real friend of mankind that this image no longer holds anything frighten-

ing for me, but is rather a source of comfort and consolation. And I thank the Lord my God that he has given me the good fortune to learn and appreciate death as the key to our true happiness. I never lie down to sleep without pondering the fact that perhaps I—young as I am—will not live to see another day. And there will not be a single man, among all those who know me, that can say that I was saddened or unwilling when my time came. And for this happiness I thank my Creator every day of my life, and from the bottom of my heart, I wish the same to every one of my fellow men."

St. Francis of Assisi died on October 3, 1226. At the age of merely 45 years, he was already an old man. He suffered from a stomach ailment that caused him to bring up blood, and he was almost blind. An attack of dropsy caused his whole body to swell painfully. St. Francis interpreted these signs correctly and composed an additional strophe for his Canticle of the Sun: "Praised be you, my Lord, in our sister the death of our body, which no human being can escape. Woe to those who die in mortal sin. Blessed is the man who is destined to rest in your most holy will; for the second death will do him no harm."

9.5 The future has already begun

9.5.0 Death, end of the line—everyone off! But what then? What is it like after death? What does the future hold for us? Is there a life after death, and is there an eternity? These questions, and questions like these, are certainly justified. But Christian faith simply refuses to peek curiously behind the scenes into the hereafter. It refuses to seek out dubious information from beyond the grave, to try to solve all the riddles. We Christians know only that there will be a judgment, a resurrection, a continued living, a heaven and a hell. As to how all this will take place, we know very little.

In Christ radiates the hope that we will rise to happiness. And even though the fate of certain death oppresses us, still we are consoled by the promise of future immortality. For in the case of your faithful, O Lord, life is changed and not taken away. And when the temporary residence of our earthly pilgrimage has been dissolved, an everlasting dwelling place is prepared in heaven (Preface for the Mass for the Dead).

9.5.1 The future: the greatest unknown. What will the future bring? The future is known to us now only in parable. But we possess magnificent promises, which allow us to anticipate indescribable joy and unhoped-for happiness. "Eye has not seen, ear has not heard, nor has it so much as dawned on man what God has prepared for those who love him" (1 Cor 2:9). "He shall wipe every tear from their eyes, and there shall be no more death or mourning, crying out or pain, for the former world has passed away" (Rv 21:4).

The promise of a new and beautiful future runs through the entire Bible: from the blessing of Abraham (Gn 12:1-3) to the Son of Man who makes all things new (Rv 21:1-5). It culminates in the promise of the new Jerusalem, in which no one will ever cry again or have to die (Rv 21:4), in which justice and peace and joy will dwell together (Is 65:17-25).

Christ is the Lord of history. He directs it. The future is his mystery. In his resurrection, time has already been fulfilled (cf. Mk 1:15; Gal 4:4-5; Heb 1:1-4). In it, our ultimate and definitive future has already dawned. This splendid future, towards which we are allowed to hope, is not the result of the great designs conceived by any human planner. No; it is the work of the love of God which embraces and transforms all things. It is the resurrection of Christ, which spans time and eternity, that transforms our life even now. And thus, our human existence is not cast into perpetual gloom by the shadow of death. Rather, it is illuminated by the light of the risen Savior.

Unfortunately, this Christian hope is not always lived as the hope of the resurrection. Perhaps we Christians need to learn, over and over again, how to dream about such a mighty hope and such a beautiful future.

9.5.2 Eternity: the eternal today of God. Here below, we humans live and think in the categories of time and space. We cannot possibly do otherwise. It is within these categories that our life and our history all play their role. In the world of God, on the other hand, there is no measurable space any more than there is any measurable time. There are no seconds and no hours, no days and no years, no sense of time with one thing following another, as here on earth. In God's eyes, a thousand years are like a single day (Ps 90:4).

This "today" of God is eternity. But eternity is not just time stretched out into endlessness. God has not developed some devilish sort of clock that keeps ticking: "Everlasting, everlasting." Eternity, however, also does not mean timelessness. It is, on the contrary, absolute mastery of time, supremacy over time, because God stands at the very center of our time and is sovereign over it. He is in no way bound to the sense of succession that characterizes our earthly time.

9.5.3 Time and eternity embrace. Christianity is a religion of the future. But "now" and "hereafter," "time" and "eternity" are not concepts that we can easily and precisely unravel from each other. Time and eternity are neither alongside each other, nor after each other, nor one above the other: they are in each other. If God is always and everywhere present, then every time and every human being and every departed human person are all "simultaneously" with God. That is what leads many theologians to speculate that our death and our resurrection, seen from a "temporal" point of view, are simultaneous. They maintain that we will rise immediately after our death.

But if we strive to place the proper emphasis on the future and eternity, we must also beware of underevaluating the here and now. Come, Lord Jesus, and delay no longer (Rv 22:20).

This coming of the Lord is not something that lies far off in the distant future. He is coming today, right now. And this waiting for him makes us restless. The Lord is near at hand, and he demands of us that we do our part: "Make the most of the present opportunity" (Ep 5:16). For the future has already been outlined for us in advance.

9.5.4 Judgment: verdict on our own heart. In his boundless love, God offers man friendship and happiness. But he does not want to force this friendship upon us. Rather, he respects the freedom of his image and likeness, of his partner. And yet, man is called by this offer of God into a decision and a judgment. Judgment is taking place right now. "Whoever does not believe is already judged" (Jn 3:18). "The man who hears my word and has faith in him who sent me possesses eternal life. . . . He has passed from death to life" (Jn 5:24). Thus, heaven and hell are already growing within the confines of our earthly life.

In death, man meets with his God definitively and for all eternity. This encounter becomes his judgment. God, of course, is not sitting in judgment over the dead person the way a human judge might do. Judgment means seeing our friendship with God in perfect clarity. It means thinking it through to its conclusion. Man sees how God has sought after him throughout his life, how he had always offered him the gift of his friendship. In this ultimate encounter, man begins to appreciate the whole measure of God's kindness and love. In this moment of truth, he will recognize who he is. All the masks will fall, all the illusions and self-deception will burst like bubbles. In the presence of God, he will suddenly comprehend what he is and what he could have been.

Friendship with God or refusal of God's friendship—this turns into our eternity. The former we call heaven, the latter hell. And thus judgment is a self-judgment at the same time that it is a judgment of God.

9.5.5 Purgatory: cleansing encounter with God. The concept of Purgatory is frequently misunderstood. Many people see it as a sort of hell of shorter duration, in which the deceased must undergo torture and punishment until he has made up for the guilt he has not atoned for during his lifetime.

But this "place of cleansing" (*purgatorium*) is not to be understood primarily as a place. Rather, it is a preliminary stage of maturing, an opportunity for man to prepare himself for the state he needs to attain before he can be admitted to the vision of God. This cleansing preparation, naturally enough, does not take place exclusively in the hereafter. It should begin here on earth. Confidence in God, penance, bearing suffering and sickness with Christian patience—all this brings us closer to the imitation of Christ.

At the moment of death, man encounters God with an intensity and profundity that he has never experienced before. This meeting with God will be his judgment, and it can be very "painful" for him. For he will recognize how lukewarm he has been in his friendship with God. And this awareness will run through him like fire, cleansing him and purifying him "like one passing through fire" (1 Cor 3:15). This cleansing, purifying process is part of Purgatory.

In this experience of cleansing, the Christian does not stand alone; he is a member of the "Communion of Saints." That is why it is a salutary idea to pray for the departed (2 M 12:38-46). It corresponds to a need within man, and also to the desire of the Christian to stay in communion with the "beloved departed." In praying for them, we must be careful to avoid any sort of counting or calculation.

9.6 "Eternally with the Lord" (1 Th 4:17)

9.6.0 The Gospels never tire of attesting, in parables and stories, to the reality of a life beyond death. What is buried in the earth at a funeral is only the earthly and perishable cloak of the man. The man himself, his central personality, lives on. As an individual human person, he remains untouched and cannot be destroyed. It is in this sense that Jesus says: "Do not fear those who deprive the body of life but cannot destroy the soul. Rather, fear him who can destroy both body and soul in Gehenna" (Mt 10:28).

St. John (Jn 4:14) speaks of a fountain which leaps up unto eternal life. In this image, the Gospel is telling us that the "eternal life" which we bear within us before our death, and the "eternal life" which we shall have after death, are not two entirely different realities. This stream of life does not simply dry up into nothingness upon our death. Rather, it continues to flow through death, into eternity.

9.6.1 Resurrection: return home and fulfillment. Death strikes the entire man. But, as we have just pointed out, the man who dies does not die away into nothingness. He enters into the eternal today of God. It is not only his soul that enters into the presence of God. Man enters into his fulfillment with his body, as well. Countless artists and lovers have sung the beauties of the human body here on earth. How incomparably more beautiful will be the glorified human body in the hereafter!

Every person is unique, one of a kind. No other person has ever loved or smiled the way we have, or spoken the way we have spoken. Only we have done the things we have done, and only we have shed tears like our tears. We all have our own individual history. And we don't simply discard all this at the moment of death. In some way we take our entire life history with us as we join with God. This too belongs to our eternity.

Every man is bound up with others: with his father, his mother, his wife, his children, his friends and relatives. All during his life, he meets many people. He looks upon many faces, and learns to know them intimately. All these acquaintances and relatives, all these people he loves are, for their part, once again bound up with other people. Every human life is made up of a network of human relationships. Through his faith, the Christian knows where he is going with his brothers and sisters. So when a believer appears before God on the occasion of his death, it is really a whole humanity, a whole history of humanity that is standing in the presence of this loving God. The human person remains oriented towards the community. Everything that he has done or embraced in love, is carried with him into the presence of his Judge and God. "Every countenance that I have loved I will find once again in you" (Ernesto Cardenal). We can hope for an eternal reunion with our beloved dead.

By his body, man is related to the earth. Chained to it and woven into it, he also carries his world into the presence of God. This and much more on the subject we find in the Bible, in its descriptions of the resurrection (Jn 5:21-30; 1 Cor 15:35-58; Ph 3:21).

9.6.2 Final judgment: Christ "all in all" (Ep 1:22-23). Again and again the Bible speaks of a "final judgment," of a "last judgment." Christ himself

(Mt 13:39-43) and St. Peter (Ac 3:21) and St. John (1 Jn 4:17) and St. Paul (2 Cor 5:10) all speak about it. On that "great day," at the end of time, Christ will come again to reveal his redemption and his friendship before all the world.

This day, too, we can predate into the world of today, here and now. The Lord is coming now; judgment is taking place now. The decisive thing is that we must here and now meet with the Lord in faith:

> I have come to rate all as loss in the light of the surpassing knowledge of my Lord Jesus Christ. For his sake I have forfeited everything; I have accounted all else rubbish so that Christ may be my wealth and I may be in him, not having any justice of my own based on observance of the law. The justice I possess is that which comes through faith in Christ. It has its origin in God and is based on faith. I wish to know Christ and the power flowing from his resurrection; likewise to know how to share in his sufferings by being formed into the pattern of his death. Thus do I hope that I may arrive at resurrection from the dead (Ph 3:8-11).

And the second most decisive element is love: "Our love is brought to perfection in this, that we should have confidence on the day of judgment; for our relation to this world is just like his. Love has no room for fear" (1 Jn 4:17-18).

9.6.3 Heaven: utopia in the hereafter? Here below we are seekers after God, always "on the move" in our faith and "on the move" towards heaven. But one day it is our hope to reach our goal and see our final longing fulfilled. We will be in heaven. But we must not picture this heaven as being some sort of utopia in the hereafter. It is more a state of being than a dwelling place. St. Paul describes it in these simple terms: "We shall be with the Lord unceasingly" (1 Th 4:17). Every attempt to grasp heaven in human words and concepts is doomed to fail. And it is just as well. We must leave it to our Lord himself to decide just how he is going to surprise us.

9.6.4 Heaven: eternal friendship. A popular song claims that friendship is too beautiful a gift for our short human life, and that there must be an eternity where friends can meet again. A person in love can, for a moment at least, be "in heaven." Genuine human love can thus be a sort of fleeting presentiment of Paradise. Heaven is something that we can only have a presentiment of. Every attempt to talk about it remains a helpless stammering. Heaven is fulfilled love; friendship turned into eternity; a final and definitive advance into the close presence of God; a never-ending meeting with God; a constant and continuous absorption into the mystery of his boundless grandeur and love; a timeless surrender to him and a beatifying sense of total immersion in the faithfulness of God. Heaven is eternally being at home with the Lord.

In this friendship, the redeemed man experiences a most profound enchantment of divine love. In the completely realized harmony between body and soul, he finds the most precious surprises of this love. Then this friendship is no longer merely an invitation and promise, but is a total fulfillment and gift. It builds up into eternal joy and gratitude. "God is greater than our heart" (1 Jn 3:20).

9.6.5 Heaven: communion of saints. "We must all come together into the presence of our dear God. What indeed would he think, if we were to come to him without the others?" (Charles Péguy). Union and friendship with Christ includes community with all his friends.

Our Lord himself speaks about heaven in parables, especially in the parable of the banquet (Lk 14:15-24) and the wedding feast (Lk 14:7-11). Heaven is the festival of love, the "Communion of saints"; it is a festival of mutual wonderment and gratitude. This means that it is anything but a self-seeking isolation of the glorified human person with his God. "We shall be his people and he will be with us" (cf. Rv 21:3).

9.6.6 Heaven: festival without bounds. We can now only begin to have a presentiment of the reality of heaven, in terms of parables and figures. In this life, we have many foreshadowings of the life that awaits us after our death. For example, honorable human love, in its capacity to give and receive, is one way that we can attain to some understanding of our life after death.

The Bible itself catalogues all our pleasant human experiences in an effort to give us, in analogies and recollections, some vague conception of heaven. It borrows comparisons from music (Rv 5:12), a new song (Rv 5:9), a beautiful garment (Is 61:10), a crown (1 Th 2:19), life (Jn 3:16), living with God (Jn 14:2), light and a city brilliant with light (Rv 22:5), the intimacy of a shared meal (Lk 14:15-24), the communal hospitality of a marriage feast (Mt 22:2-14), the security of a child whose mother wipes away his tears (Rv 21:4), and the blessedness of earthly love (1 Cor 2:9). In heaven there will be no blind or lame, no lepers or dead. There will be untroubled joy, and no place any more for suffering, sickness or death (Rv 21:4). The most blessed element, of course, will be the vision and knowledge of God (1 Cor 13:12; 1 Jn 3:2). To sum it all up, heaven is a kingdom of freedom and joy, reconciliation and justice, friendship turned into eternity, festival without bounds.

9.6.7 Hell: friendship refused. Talking about hell is even more difficult than talking about heaven. Hell is the exact opposite of heaven. The eternal damnation of a human person, and the boundless love of God, are not in themselves a contradiction in terms. For, in the last analysis, it is not God who damns anyone to hell. Rather, the human person damns himself. The punishment of hell is not an act of vengeance on the part of an all-merciful and good God. Hell is nothing more than the most extreme and logical consequence of God's love face to face with human evil and ill will.

God loves everyone on earth, and it is his will to save them all. He encourages the sinner to conversion. Up to the very last moment, he offers him his mercy and his friendship. But he does not force his friendship upon anyone. He respects the freedom of the human will. But even the greatest love is powerless if it is rejected and denied. Thus if anyone, acting with clear knowledge and complete freedom, were to reject God's free offer of his friendship, and if this consciously willed split with God were to persevere up to the very moment of death, then this act of rejection would take on a final and decisive validity. God respects this free decision, this final refusal on the part of men. He tells him, at the hour of his death, "Your will be done." God's love and his loving justice do not contradict each other at all, and they can never mutually exclude each other.

Damnation, in the last analysis, is a case of man damning himself. And this self-judgment on the part of man is at the same time a judgment of God. After all the injustice of this world, there must be, at least in the hereafter, a perfect justice.

The terrible words "Depart from me!" (Mt 25:41) are the echo of Jesus' neglected call to repentance. Hell is sin and rejection of God turned into eternity. It is God's eternally present love that makes up hell for the damned soul. This love will burn forever, because the man in hell will always experience this love as something very near at hand, and will still always reject it. This is hell: endless removal from God, together with endless nostalgia for him. And thus hell itself is a demonstration of the ultimate seriousness of God's offer of his salvific friendship. When Jesus speaks of hell, he never describes it. In his proclamations, he is concerned with the earnestness of the present moment of decision. In images of fire that is never quenched, of the worm that never dies, of eternal darkness, of howling and gnashing of teeth—this is how he alludes to the possibility of a once-and-for-all rejection of God.

9.7 The "new earth" (2 P 3:13)

9.7.0 Earth belongs to man. Its fate is linked intimately with his own. Our conceptions of the world have been fundamentally altered. Even today, no one knows precisely how the earth came into being. But we do know that our earth is only an insignificant bit of dust, a mere particle of the universe. It circles around the sun, and courses along on its way through the universe. It has taken millions and millions of years for the earth to develop. After a lengthy cycle of evolution had created the necessary prerequisites, plants and animals developed a manifold network of ecological interconnections. In the midst of all this man has been deposited, the most recent inhabitant of our earth. He is capable of asserting mastery over all of it. But he is also capable of so abusing it that he himself may someday no longer be able to live. The development continues. Creation is not yet finished.

9.7.1 Earth—where to? On the morning of creation, the Lord put everything into motion. Since that time, the world has been subjected to transformation and development. The cosmos is a bold plan which has succeeded admirably. The adventure of creation is an age-long development towards its ultimate fulfillment. Where and how and when it will all end, no one knows.

The risk we take with the world is worth the effort. Our faith tells us that the earth is intimately bound up with Christ. The redemption of man cannot take place without the redemption of the universe. "Indeed, the whole created world eagerly awaits the revelation of the sons of God. . . . The world itself will be freed from its slavery to corruption and share in the glorious freedom of the children of God" (Rm 8:19, 21).

The Letter to the Colossians has some unexpectedly bold assertions: "Everything was created through him and for him. In him everything continues in being" (Col 1:16-17). To sum it up in a few words, the adventure of creation, and thus also of our earth, begins with Christ and ends with him as well.

9.7.2 Not the end of the world, but its fulfillment. We often speak of the end of the world or of the destruction of the world. These expressions can be easily misunderstood. What we are talking about here is not an end at

all, but rather a transformation and a fulfillment. Christianity is a religion which is oriented towards the future.

Now, it is true that the Bible describes, in apocalyptic imagery, how the world is going to experience a series of catastrophes before its ultimate fulfillment (Mk 13). St. Paul, for his part, writes that the present world is passing away (1 Cor 7:31). But the world as such will not pass away. Instead of speaking about the end of the world, the Bible speaks about a new beginning. "What we await are new heavens and a new earth, where, according to his promise, the justice of God will reside" (2 P 3:13). According to the Book of Revelation, this new beginning is the work of the risen and glorified Savior: "Then I saw new heavens and a new earth. The former heavens and the former earth had passed away. . . . The One who sat upon the throne said to me: Behold, I make all things new" (Rv 21:1, 5).

9.7.3 New creation in Christ. Christ is, accordingly, "the beginning of the new creation," "the foundation of the new world"; "in him" and "through him" and "unto him" all things have been created. Creation has "its whole being in him." He "holds together everything in heaven and on earth" (Col 1:17) within himself. To put it in other words: "Christ's resurrection is the beginning of the final glorification of the world. Creation too, in its essential elements, has risen with him.

Easter began this "new creation" (2 Cor 5:17). It will be completed only when it enters into final glory with Christ. Creation and redemption mutually complement and fulfill one another.

For Christ, the resurrection did not involve any dissolution from the world, but rather a new relationship of closeness to the world and to all mankind. So we have a right to hope that our life in heaven will involve a deeper relationship with the world. The earth and all the universe as well, will be a part of our heaven.

9.8 Faith in today

9.8.0 There are two days in every week, writes an anonymous sage, about which we are not supposed to be concerned. These two days are to be kept free of fear and anxiety.

One of these days is yesterday, with all its mistakes and problems, its errors and missed opportunities. All the money in the world cannot bring yesterday back.

The other day is tomorrow, with all its potential unpleasantness, its burdens and big promises and (often) small accomplishments. Tomorrow is outside of our immediate control. The sun will rise tomorrow morning, either in all its beauty or behind a veil of clouds. But it will surely rise. Until it does, we have no claim upon tomorrow, for the new day is as yet unborn.

That leaves us only one day, today. Everyone can face the struggles of only one day with some kind of success. Let us then concern ourselves only with that which we can face and deal with successfully. Let us apply all our energies to today.

9.8.1 Today of God—today of faith. Our Church and our faith are also subject to the laws of history. The Christian lives in the tension between the first appearance of Christ and his final coming at the end of time. And thus, he can neither cling spasmodically to the past, nor dream contentedly of the future. He has to live in, believe in, and address himself to the present. For it is now that Christ lives, and this is the "acceptable time, the day of salvation" (2 Cor 6:2). Let us "make the most of the present opportunity" (Ep 5:16).

9.8.2 Grave watchers? We are all familiar with the scene described in the Gospel (Mt 28). On Easter morning, Jesus rises from the dead and appears to his disciples. They are filled with joy and renewed hope. At the same time, there are still a few men keeping watch before the empty grave. While the Lord is alive, they are guarding what they think is a corpse, with deadly earnest. They are all concerned about the dead. Then these grave-watchers realize the true state of things. Their reaction is well-known. They look for scapegoats: "His disciples have stolen the body" (Mt 28:13). And their deceit lives on after them: "This is the story that circulates among the Jews to this very day" (Mt 28:15). In our day too, there are many Christians, even priests and religious, who imitate these grave-watchers. They are all involved with Christ, but not with the living Christ of today who is with us in our modern world. Instead of believing that the Resurrection points to the future, they commit themselves to the past. They are walking backwards while looking into the future. They have fallen victim to an unhealthy wave of nostalgia. They limp along behind, yapping at the wheels of progress in world and Church alike. Christ, alive in the spirit of our modern time, gives us hope and a future. God is not to be found in the cemetery of history, nor in the waiting room of the future: he is here today.

9.8.3 Courage for today. Truly, no man should feel so passionately involved with the present as the Christian. "Pay attention to the present

time; accommodate yourself to the conditions of each passing moment"
(Rule of Taizé).

The style and manner in which faith responds will vary considerably,
following changes in society, psychology, and customs. Deep-seated
transformations can be very disquieting. That is understandable. But this
is the situation that true faith must learn to accept. "If the intellectual
situation of today demands this particular sort of faith from us, then we
have no grounds to be uncertain about it" (K. Rahner). We must not fall
victim to a sort of pathological anxiety and sense of intimidation. Our faith
is not something that we have to defend against a whole series of
difficulties and threats. Neither do we have to save our faith. It is supposed to save us. Only the dead never change. Where there is life, there
is also change and activity. In our faith, we can also have confidence in
history. This alone will preclude any sort of "catastrophe mentality." We
shall believe only in love, and no longer be astonished at anything.

9.8.3 "Dynamic of the current." Historical change has, today, violently
touched the Church and her understanding of the faith. It sometimes
seems that everything is in a state of flux. It is our mission to distinguish
between what is abiding and what is capable of undergoing historical
development. Many forms were good in one particular era. But now it
would be meaningless to cling to outmoded forms, or to defend them as a
matter of life and death. Much of what passes for the rejection of faith is,
in reality, only the rejection of obsolete historical forms. Our faith demands that we show a degree of flexibility in these matters, and exercise
the "dynamic of the current." We always have to reevaluate the signs of
the times and must always remain open to new historical goals.

No generation can claim that it alone has wholly understood and
realized the cause of Jesus. The Church is and remains a Church of
discussion and adaptation. But the Lord is the same today and yesterday
and tomorrow!

CONCLUSION:

ARRIVING AT THE GOAL

9.9 Mary: a model of faith

9.9.0 We are not Mary-worshippers. We know that she is a creature like us. She is from the same frail human stock as you and I. She came into the world a defenseless child, just like us. As a human being, she was capable of joy and sorrow. She is neither a goddess nor a superwoman. She is wholly and completely one of us, at our side.

9.9.1 *"Let it be done to me as you say" (Lk 1:38)*. The most striking element in the life of this woman is not her magnificent privilege, but rather her unshakable faith. We often like to suppose that Mary had an easy time of it with her faith. But the contrary is true. Like everyone else, she had to struggle along her pilgrimage of faith. But in her union with Christ, she held firm all the way to Good Friday.

In the fullness of time, God sends a messenger to this Jewish maiden of Nazareth. The message is an amazing one. In a boldly calculated risk, God is going to entrust his only Son to this young maiden, for her to prepare a body for him in her womb. The reaction of this believing mortal is very comforting. Mary is frightened (Lk 1:29). She is confused by the nearness of God, and wonders what it all means (Lk 1:29). She has questions to ask (Lk 1:34). Faith does not have to be unquestioning, accepting everything blindly and leaving the thinking to someone else. Mary is not forced. God's first word to Mary is a greeting. The angel's message is an invitation. And Mary allows herself to be moved by the words of God. She does not refuse; in her faith, she gives a truly splendid answer: "I am the servant of the Lord. Let it be done to me as you say" (Lk 1:38).

She gives in completely to God. "Let it be done to me as you say." In that very moment, Mary becomes the partner of the Lord. With these words, she consents to a way of faith that still appears unclear and very dark to her. She gives her assent to a life of testing, in which her faith will be tried again and again.

She gives birth to her child in a shepherd's stall. And he is supposed to be the infinite God, the Creator of heaven and earth.

With Jesus and Joseph she flees into exile in Egypt, because a tyrant is trying to kill her child. And this fugitive baby is supposed to be the almighty God.

Thirty years later, this young man Jesus is condemned to death. Mary meets the despised criminal along the way of the cross. She sees him streaming with blood, cruelly whipped along the path to his place of punishment. On Golgotha she listens and watches as they drive nails into her son's body and raise him up on the shameful gibbet of the cross. Then Jesus bleeds to death, in indescribable agony on Calvary. And this man hanging on a cross is supposed to be the Redeemer of all mankind, the King of all nations, and the Lord of history. Mary experiences the silence of God. Nothing is spared her. And this believing woman has the courage to stand beneath the cross; she stands by the crucified Savior. His disciples abandon him. But Mary does not prove false to him in this terrible hour. She has faith.

9.9.2 "The Lord is with you" (Lk 1:28). Faith is friendship. Mary must have experienced this fact as no one else ever has. She bore within her womb the Son of God as her own son. She might well have wondered at this singular privilege: "God who is mighty has done great things for me" (Lk 1:49).

Let us imagine what must have gone through her mind at this moment:

"My forebears have told me that you are so exalted above everything that exists that I dare not even pronounce your name, that I will die if I presume to approach your presence. And now, you yourself have made your way into the narrow confines of my womb. In me, you have sunk your roots as a human person. In me, you have taken a new name, Emmanuel, God with us. That you are, my Child.

"My people Israel have experienced your mighty deeds from generation to generation. You were with Israel. You guided her and set her free. Our fathers have told me the wonderful story of your love. And now this history has actually taken on human flesh within me. I am privileged to bear within myself both the memory of your many great works, and also the fulfillment of your unheard-of promises.